S0-ACA-288

THE NEW AMERICAN COMMUNITY

THE NEW
AMERICAN COMMUNITY

A Response to the European
and Asian Economic Challenge

Jerry M. Rosenberg

New York
Westport, Connecticut
London

FLORIDA STATE
UNIVERSITY LIBRARIES

HC
94
R67
1992

NOV 19 1992

TALLAHASSEE, FLORIDA

Library of Congress Cataloging-in-Publication Data

Rosenberg, Jerry Martin.
    The new American community : a response to the European and Asian
economic challenge / Jerry M. Rosenberg.
      p. cm.
    Includes bibliographical references and index.
    ISBN 0–275–94206–6 (alk. paper)
    1. America—Economic integration. 2. Free trade—America.
3. International economic integration. 4. International trade.
5. Commercial treaties. I. Title.
HC94.R67 1992
337.1'7—dc20   91–35038

British Library Cataloguing in Publication Data is available.

Copyright © 1992 by Jerry M. Rosenberg

All rights reserved. No portion of this book may be
reproduced, by any process or technique, without the
express written consent of the publisher.

Library of Congress Catalog Card Number: 91-35038
ISBN: 0–275–94206–6

First published in 1992

Praeger Publishers, One Madison Avenue, New York, NY 10010
An imprint of Greenwood Publishing Group, Inc.

Printed in the United States of America

The paper used in this book complies with the Permanent
Paper Standard issued by the National Information Standards
Organization (Z39.48—1984).

10 9 8 7 6 5 4 3 2 1

This book is affectionately dedicated to
Ellen
For thirty-one years together she has unselfishly
shared her love, wisdom, and know-how

"From the Old World to the New World,
then to the New-Old-World, and now,
back to the New-New-World"

CONTENTS

PREFACE

The story has often been told that after bombing Pearl Harbor on December 7, 1941, the victorious Japanese pilots surrounded their greatly respected Admiral Yamamoto who, instead of celebrating, was in a momentary state of despair. "Why are you not happy?" he was asked, only to reply that in attacking the Americans he knew he had stirred the "sleeping giant."

Global events of the 1990s will thrust Americans into a new mood of excitement, energy, and pride. The "sleeping giant" will once again respond with vigor and vitality. Having just completed a book, *The New Europe*, covering the European Community, I became convinced that the United States' preoccupation with Japan during the 1980s left it severely handicapped in comprehending the goals and regulations of the post–1992 projections for Europe. Now begins the Americas' moment of catching up, poised for a spirited challenge—the renewed prosperity from free trade.

Contrary to what some may think, NAC will not stand, in the long run, for North American Community, but New American Community. I sincerely believe that in due time the future will bring first a North American advance that will ultimately be integrated with a Central- and South-American commitment to an era of free enterprise, without trade and fiscal barriers.

To be sure, bilateral and regional trade agreements can unlock enormous economic benefits, where it is expected that workers of the United States, Canada, and Mexico will see their incomes expand anywhere from

2 to 8 percent as a result of North American free trade agreements. But the benefits of bilateral free trade aren't necessarily additive. In addition, this kind of arrangement would be very complex, since different rules would be negotiated to deal with the particular circumstances of different nations.

There is a better long-term approach, that is, the New American Community—a regional agreement for all of the Americas. When modeled, in part, after Europe 1992, with all its pitfalls and fantasies, it could avoid the kind of problems that a series of bilateral treaties would create.

On one hand, I could have a guilt hangover for borrowing extensively from European Community publications and from materials distributed at E.C. meetings I've attended, all of which required years of mental anguish and effort to evolve via debate and trial. On the other hand, in the preparation of this document, comparisons with the creative efforts around the globe have convinced me of the E.C.'s significant contribution and application to the needs of a New American Community.

Of course, enormous hurdles exist for the NAC, indeed many far greater than those of the 12 member states of the European Community. The nations of the western hemisphere don't automatically form a natural match. Nearly all are debtor nations and need to raise their exports relative to the rest of the world to balance their books.

Likewise, an intensive examination of the motivations, strategies, and goals of Japan have further reinforced my awareness of the critical path the United States must follow to avoid a further withering of our living standard. The Pacific Rim countries, with their different cultures and histories, have piloted a course of investment and economic creativity that can be refreshing and useful in preparing within the Americas for the new millennium. We all can learn much from the strengths, convictions, and accomplishments demonstrated by the peoples of these nations, some of which should become a model for incorporation into the New American Community, some of which to be rejected following careful analysis.

Yes, there remains the continuing fear of increased military tension throughout the Americas. However, South America has undergone a change as dramatic as found in Eastern Europe over the past decade, only it was missed or minimized by the media.

A few years ago, military men were in power in almost all of South America. Armed forces were geared toward fighting internal subversion. Border conflicts flared. Today, democracy is largely the rule. The idea of open borders and economic integration is catching on throughout the region. And yet, there remains a lingering mistrust between armed forces and civilian governments that reign throughout South America, testing the solidity of the democratic revolution that swept the region in the past few years.

The struggle to democratize remains the only possible way to give the masses a higher living standard in countries south of the U.S. border. The New American Community will prove to be the primary tool to raise hopes and aspirations to a point of economic, social, and political reality. Frequently, experiments with institutions can improve the lives of more people than efforts of individual ambition, which can fray when faced with organizational obstacles. The chance the New American Community will have for success involves a significant degree of mutual trust and influence among NAC nations.

On a personal level, this manuscript completes a major cycle. In 1957, the year the Treaty of Rome was signed creating the European Common Market, I was awarded a Fulbright and French Government Scholarship and studied in Paris; I taught in Rome, Italy the year that the Single European Act was implemented; this book is published in 1992—the year of the fall of trade barriers for the 12 member states of the European Community; and a renewed spirit and interest begins in the future of the new world—the Americas, discovered by explorers from the old world in 1492.

My immediate family continues to be an inspiration for this pursuit. Ellen, my wife, and children Liz, Lauren, and Robert have throughout the time spent on this work offered their love and support. In addition, special thanks to James R. Dunton, Editor-in-Chief at Praeger for his thoughtful and professional approach in seeing this book reach publication.

Lastly, it was with great pride to have been invited to the University of the Yucatan in Merida, Mexico where I delivered my first presentation on the New American Community on January 11, 1991.

INTRODUCTION

If the Europeans after 2,000 years of killing each other, have found a way
to understand each other, then so can Central Americans, Mexicans, and
North Americans.
> —Octavio Paz, winner, 1990 Nobel Prize in Literature (written
> following a study of Europe's integration prospects after 1992)

The focus for the remainder of this century and far into the new millennium
will be the globalization of trade and commerce. Over the past several
decades strategies have been implemented and the outcome has been the
surfacing of a division of the world into three strong, competing economic
forces; the European Sector, the Asian Sector, and the American Sector.
Other nations, including so-called third world countries will be compass
points facing decisions about which point in the triangle to favor. For
some it will be a singular response, for others, attempts will be made to
secure a sound and profitable footing with all three sources of opportunity.

A more careful expansion from the core of these three sectors reveals
a blossoming fringe purporting to associate itself with a nucleus, to ride
on the coattails of an already prosperous economy, envisioning a far
greater abundance within a region. In brief, the triangle of global commerce can be described as follows.

1. The European Sector commences with the European Community,
but expands swiftly to include the nations of the European Free Trade
Association, then Central and Eastern Europe. Combined, they total a
population in excess of 520 million.

2. The Asian Sector, with a population of 145 million, has Japan as its nucleus but on the periphery, and coming on strong, are countries of EANIC. Standing by with high hopes are China and other neighbors.

3. The American Sector has at its focal center the United States, forming a North American Community with its boundary neighbors Canada and Mexico, and a combined population of more than 360 million. Not far away, well planted in the wings of opportunity are countries from both Central and South America, along with Caribbean states. The Latin American component combined with the northern hemisphere unite to embrace the New American Community with a total of more than 700 million people.

The present day realities of trade and commerce among these units are staggering, and when presented with a future of friction, protectionism, tariffs, quotas, etc., the counter challenge is a race for free trade, an advanced living standard, supremacy, quality, recognition, and power.

And so an ever-expanding or even a declining economy, will always be a slicing up of the pie, shares distributed among the aggressive, fortunate, magnetic, and progressive nations willing to push and pull hard to dominate. The descriptive triangle in Figure 1 illustrates the present state of affairs. For no reason other than pride, the United States appears at the top (along with other western hemisphere nations), but the equality of the pyramid permits a rotation in any direction. Confidence should not be based on patriotism but, instead, earned.

Trade wars and protectionism, accompanied by a fluctuating value of the dollar will continue to impact on the export success of U.S. businesses. Several years ago when the dollar was strong, U.S. exports dropped and the United States had a surplus with the rest of Europe and Japan. When the U.S. Department of Commerce released its 1990 trade results in February 1991, the merchandise trade deficit overall persisted at a level of $101 billion for the year. However, for the first time since 1983, the United States had a surplus in merchandise trade with 23 countries of Western Europe, who consume nearly 30 percent of America's exports. United States firms sold $4 billion more to Europe in 1990 than they bought. Exports to Europe, at a 13 percent increase, outstripped export rises to Japan, Canada, and the rest of the world.

The U.S., long derided as an industrial failure, has ever so gradually become one of the globe's low-cost manufacturers—lower in many industries than Japan and Europe. Our exports, in late spring 1991, had surged by 76 percent since 1986. Four years later the percentage increase in our top five exports were: aircraft—99.4 percent, electrical machinery—133.1 percent, cars and trucks—61.4 percent, computers and office machines—69.5 percent, and small manufactured goods—145.9 percent; a set of very impressive statistics. The jump in exports and sinking demand for imports narrowed the nation's trade deficit in March 1991 to $4.05

Figure 1

The New American Community (NAC)

NORTH AMERICA — Total Population: 362 million,
GNP: $5.9 trillion, Trade: $225 billion

CENTRAL AMERICA — (7 nations) Total Population: 28 million
CARIBBEAN — Population: 30 million
SOUTH AMERICA — (13 nations) Population: 280 million

TOTAL POPULATION
700 million

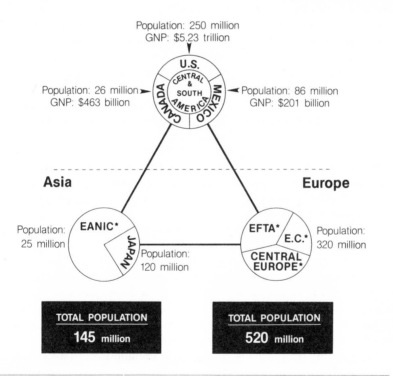

Population: 250 million
GNP: $5.23 trillion

U.S.
CENTRAL & SOUTH AMERICA
CANADA
MEXICO

Population: 26 million
GNP: $463 billion

Population: 86 million
GNP: $201 billion

Asia

Europe

EANIC*
JAPAN

Population: 25 million

Population: 120 million

EFTA*
E.C.*
CENTRAL EUROPE*

Population: 320 million

TOTAL POPULATION
145 million

TOTAL POPULATION
520 million

---

* **GNP** – Gross National Product
EFTA – European Free Trade Association: Norway, Sweden, Finland, Austria, Switzerland & Iceland
CENTRAL EUROPE – (Eastern) Bulgaria, Czechoslovakia, Hungary, Poland, Romania & Yugoslavia
E.C. – European Community: Belgium, Denmark, France, Germany, Greece, Ireland, Italy,
Luxembourg, Netherlands, Portugal, Spain & United Kingdom
EANIC – East Asian Newly Industrialized Countries: Hong Kong, Singapore, South Korea & Taiwan

billion, the smallest monthly imbalance in almost eight years. By comparison, the deficit totaled $5.5 billion in February and $8.62 billion in March of 1990.

Once again we are competitive, as our export-led growth becomes our future's strategy with a weakened dollar and lower production costs. For example, the average cost of producing a ton of U.S. steel is about $535 compared to $542 in Germany and $614 in Japan.

The pendulum can swing in favor of the western hemisphere's abundant natural resources, technology, and selective wages. Even were the dollar to strengthen, as it will periodically, we can still surge ahead in the world. While Americans presently earn $14.31 an hour in pay and benefits, German workers earn $17.58. In Japan, where pay has more than doubled in dollar terms since 1979, workers now earn the equivalent of $12.63 an hour and it is increasing rapidly. Whether in Mexico, Central America, or South America, wages will for a long period remain but a fraction of those in the States, and will be one of the incentives where all can benefit. This may only be the beginning for the United States, working in close cooperation with Canada, Mexico, and then eventually on a united front with the Central and South American nations. We will all move forward, determined to hold steady to our course. Only a prepared and united New American Community can prosper if there is a willingness to sacrifice and work for this distinguished future.

Protectionism no longer protects. Protectionism stifles. Protectionists argue of lost jobs and lower wages, but the opposite usually follows. Many firms survive thanks to overseas subsidiaries, bringing greater abundance and higher salaries. Free-trade agreements will lead the way for increased prosperity.

The New American Community will not support protectionism, nor will it accept the standard description of regionalism. Indeed, as the world consolidates into three free-trading blocs, the existence of the NAC will encourage the move to grander levels of open world markets. The potentials for retaliation and counter-retaliation must be eliminated. At all times, the classic problems facing the NAC—that of diverting trade from efficient nonmembers to less efficient members—will be a constant reminder of the difficulties to be anticipated in its creation.

The concepts for the New American Community extend beyond The Enterprise for the Americas Initiative proposed by President Bush in a major policy address in Washington on June 27, 1990. While the outline for the New American Community deals with major policy proposals of trade, investment, and debt, as does The Enterprise for the Americas Initiative, it reaches further to include a formal treaty, structural and legal aspects, the elimination of fiscal barriers, hemispheric channels for upgraded education, means for industrial cooperation, efforts in health protection, a common market for a broad set of services, coordinated research and development efforts, the setting of common standards, and the establishment of a charter of social rights for all.

The chapters ahead describe the evolution of the New American Community, of the United States, Canada, Mexico, and Latin America, with its enormous hemispheric population of 719 million people and an impressive gross domestic product of $6.8 trillion.

Chapters 1–4 present a historical picture of the multivarying forces from across both of our boundary waters that have forced the Americas into their present predicament and challenge. Chapters 5–6 deal with the international trade and legislative components that necessitate an independent move by the Americas. Chapters 7–9 develop the formal structure, including a treaty and legal procedure for the New American Community. Chapters 10–17 point in specific terms to the areas where study, negotiations, and change will be required before a secure New American Community can prosper. Chapter 18 concludes this vision of hope for the Americas with a restatement of principle and determination.

1

ACROSS THE ATLANTIC

While the U.S. government continues to be preoccupied with deficits and the impact of a recession, and while investors face up to a volatile stock market producing fears of future economic disarray, nations of the European Community, the European Free Trade Association, and Central Europe, with a population of 520 million, are redefining what in the 1990s is meant by "economic cooperation."

THE EUROPEAN COMMUNITY

The 12 member nations of the European Community have forged ahead toward achieving the goal of internal integration. Europe 1992 was designed by Europe for Europeans, so that European companies would profit from subsidies and protectionism. The economies of these countries, with their long history of political conflict, will be merged into a large free-trade region. The political fission and economic integration reflect two trends: declining advantages of the large nation-state and increased gains from access to bigger markets. Foreign fears of a Fortress Europe surrounded by one effective tariff wall, rather than numerous smaller ones, become real. Not since Napoleon's quest to unite Europe has anything so ambitious been attempted.

The stakes are high. The Community's gross national product of $4.46 trillion accounts for 20 percent of world output—more than the United States. The U.S. stake in Europe's plan is also huge. The European Community is America's chief trading partner, accounting for $145 billion annually in combined exports and imports, more than either Canada or Japan. Including the output of U.S.-owned companies in Europe and European-owned firms in the U.S., the size of the relationship is $1 trillion a year.

United States–European Community trade in 1990 represented 36 percent of world trafficking of goods and services, with a total investment of $280 billion. American exports to the European Community were more than $60 billion, with imports nearly $85 billion, producing a U.S. deficit of $24.3 billion.

By the late 1980s, U.S. trade with the E.C. nations totaled $132.6 billion, approximately one-fifth of all U.S. trade, but the U.S. retained a $26 billion trade deficit. The E.C.'s share of U.S. exports has fallen from 35 percent to about 18 percent, with member states of the European Community capturing many of our former markets around the globe.

To a great extent, the E.C.'s aggressive strategies have confused the world's supply-demand equilibrium, largely at U.S. expense. For example, by the late 1980s the E.C. had replaced the U.S. as the primary producer of numerous commodities:

—the E.C. is the world's largest dairy exporter, accounting for 60 percent of the trade. European Community imports of processed fruit and vegetable products are negligible, while exports of canned fruit penetrate foreign markets.

—the E.C.'s wheat and flour exports increased fivefold since the mid-1970s, to an estimated 17 million metric tons. It is now the world's third largest wheat exporter.

—prior to the mid 1970s, the E.C. was a net importer of beef and veal. Now it is the world's largest exporter.

—the E.C. is presently the world's largest egg exporter, shipping 2.7 billion eggs a year. Before 1967, it was the world's largest egg importer.

—by the mid-1960s, the E.C. was the world's largest importer of poultry products and is now the globe's largest exporter, accounting for 36 percent of the world's chicken business.

From E.C. headquarters in Brussels a White Paper was published in June 1985 defining the European Community's Commission program for "Completing the Internal Market," listing over 300 (eventually reduced to 282) legislative proposals and a timetable for their adoption. The internal market referred to all related activities with the 12 member states (Belgium, Denmark, France, Germany, Greece, Ireland, Italy, Luxembourg, Netherlands, Portugal, Spain, and the United Kingdom). The White Paper was soon endorsed by the Heads of States and Government. The aim was to weld together the 12 separate national economies into a single market of 330 million people—a single Europe by the end of 1992.

The White Paper was given a constitutional basis by the Single European Act, becoming a major amendment to the 1957 Treaty of Rome that had given birth to the Common Market. It was passed to facilitate the adoption of the White Paper measures by December 31, 1992. The Act adapted the Community's procedures for decision making and increased the scope for a type of majority (as opposed to unanimous) voting in the Council of Ministers. It became effective on July 1, 1987, and was ratified by the Parliaments of all member states. It significantly improved the institutional system by setting new objectives for the Community, notably the completion of the internal market, "an area without internal frontiers in which the free movements of goods, persons, services and capital is ensured in accordance with provisions of this Treaty" by 1992 and the strengthening of economic and social cohesion, without internal frontiers.

The European Community's best kept secret is its most threatening weapon. In only a few years, the 12 member states have been planning a strategy, in part already operational, to take on the United States, and more specifically, Japan. The stage for conflict between the European Community and the United States is set. A tug of war between us may rupture many of our common bonds. "A friend for ever," will be severely tested when Americans feel the pinch of an eventually lowered standard. Fingers may well point to the new antagonists across the Atlantic, creating the potential for a long struggle for supremacy, prestige, and a new meaning of "survival."

The R & D Factories

The European Community and member governments are releasing billions of dollars for their megaresearch programs. Within the next five years, along with company resources, about $16 billion will be used to develop high-tech research and their resulting family of products. With new E.C. directives, revised tax laws will allow greater expansion into the venture capital markets, resulting in Europe surpassing the $2.5 billion the United States spent in 1988.

As an indication of their research and development strength, the European Community combines people, talents, ambitions, and resources to assert its determined leadership in science and technology. Special areas of development include overall research, the computer challenge, industrial applications, and the telecommunications complex.

Overall Research

Since the early 1980s the European Community has thrown vast quantities of funds and manpower into modernizing its scientific base. A host of programs have emerged, many of them borrowing from existing U.S. technologies. In the late 1970s the European Community established the

European Science Foundation (it was modeled after the U.S. National Science Foundation) linking the national research programs of sixteen nations. Its primary goal is to promote collaboration in research, to encourage mobility among research workers, to assist the exchange of information and ideas among participating nations, and to encourage the harmonizing of research activities and programs.

Further coordination was needed. Forecasting and Assessment in the field of Science and Technology (FAST), was adopted in 1978. Its main goal is to define long-term research and development priorities for the Community on the basis of which new Community research programs can be planned. FAST is a shared-cost research program involving numerous research and forecasting centers in the Community, with activities focusing on the relations between technology, work and employment, the transformation of services, the communication function, the future of the food system, and integrated development of renewable natural resources.

The Single European Act of 1987 led to the creation of a European Research and Technology Community, giving the Community specific powers in the field of scientific and technical cooperation forming a basis for the framework program of research and technological development through 1991, and of course, beyond. Its present eight primary areas of action are: quality of life, dealing with health (cancer and AIDS are emphasized), radiation protection and the environment; information technology and telecommunications; industrial technologies of manufacturing, advanced materials, raw materials, and technical standards and reference materials; biological resources including biotechnology, energy including thermonuclear fusion, radioactive waste management and storage, the decommissioning and dismantling of nuclear facilities; science and technology for development; marine resources; and European scientific and technical cooperation.

SCIENCE, the Stimulation of the International Cooperation and Interchange Need by European Research Scientists, was adopted in the summer of 1988. SCIENCE promotes the exchange of research workers within the European Community and finances research projects, twin laboratories in different member states, and provides grants to researchers to enable them to work in European Community countries other than their own.

To deal with research in nuclear energy, solar energy, and related matters, a Joint Research Center (JRC) was created with its four establishments at Ispra in Italy, Karlsruhe in the Federal Republic of Germany, Geel in Belgium, and Petten in The Netherlands.

Located in Culham, England, JET, the Joint European Torus, is a doughnut-shaped vacuum vessel for creating inexpensive, clean energy by the fusion of hydrogen atoms, as on the sun's surface. The objective is to construct such an experimental vessel large enough to study a plasma in conditions simulating those in a thermonuclear project.

SPRINT, the Strategic Program for Innovation and Technology Transfer was adopted in the summer of 1988 to reinforce and add a new dimension to the E.C.'s activities. SPRINT is an important element within the framework of the E.C.'s research and development aspirations to master technological change, lying in the heart of the technological transformation of the European economy. A second phase concentrates on: strengthening the European infrastructure for innovation services by forming or consolidating intra-E.C. networks of technology transfer and innovation support professionals, supporting pilot projects on innovation transfer that focus on the application of existing technologies to receptive sectors, improving the environment for innovation by making the process involved better known, and increasing coordination between the member states and the E.C. Commission.

COMETT, the Community Program in Education and Training for Technology, provides a favorable environment for the assimilation and diffusion of new technologies and strengthens links between higher education institutions and the business sector. $258 million have been set aside for this effort until 1995.

The Computer Challenge

Europe's computer industry is stirring from a long slumber. The home market for hardware doubled to $38 billion from 1980 to 1985. On the software market, the E.C. calculated orders at $25 million in 1987 and predicts a market size of $58 million for 1992. The largest segment, the standard package software market, shows the fastest growth—24 percent in 1987.

Several E.C. companies plan to spend vast amounts of money on JESSI, the Joint European Submicron Silicon, a program to develop future member chips, with the E.C. and various governments paying half the costs. By June 1989 the E.C. threw its weight behind this $4 billion research and development program. With $500 million annually, it is funded at twice that of Sematech, a comparable U.S. consortium.

ESPRIT, the European Strategic Program for Research and Development in Information Technology, was launched in 1984. It involves work on mini-supercomputers: work on improving industrial production by getting computers to communicate with each other; computer systems that will be able to control equipment and appliances in private homes; and establishing Europe-wide software certification procedures and developing computerized work stations that simultaneously use voice, writing, data, and charts. Within the ESPRIT projects all the major European manufacturers are joining forces to make sure that their computers link up easily. ESPRIT II, approved in 1988, now has nearly 450 contracts funded with $5 billion until 1993, of which half will be provided by the E.C. for work on computer-aided design standards, communication networks for manufacturing applications, etc.

Euronet Diane, the Direct Information Access Network for Europe was created in the early 1980s as an information service with a special transmission network (Euronet) linking London, Paris, Rome, Frankfurt, Dublin, Brussels, Amsterdam, Luxembourg, and Copenhagen. It is composed of independent European computerized information services that can give access to databases and data banks on numerous subjects. It is Europe's first high-speed, computerized information retrieval system. Initially, 40 host computers gave access to over 300 data banks covering a wide variety of scientific, technical, social, and economic information. Over 2,300 companies and organizations use this system.

CERN, the European Organization for Nuclear Research, based in Geneva, has the European Laboratory for Particle Physics, a 14-nation $700 million supercollider project that built the world's largest atom smasher, the 17 mile-long Large Electron-Positron Collider.

Industrial Applications

BRITE, the Basic Research in Industrial Technology in Europe project was launched in 1985 as a program to increase the use of advanced technologies in the traditional sectors of industry. Research is designed to be precompetitive in nature, with commercial product development being left entirely to industry. Projects were developed that parallel many U.S. efforts, covering a wide range of industrial disciplines, often making surprising use of techniques developed in one area to make new applications in another, and a few key technological fields (including laser technology, membrane science, catalysis and particle technology, and new material joining techniques) have been priorities. Under the first phase of the BRITE program, 1,000 firms, research centers, and universities have worked on 200 projects. $722 million have been allocated to 1992.

EUREKA, a type of ad hoc industrial policy of the E.C., was founded in 1988. The program sponsors 302 non-defense joint projects at a cost exceeding $10 billion (including $4 billion for the JESSI semiconductor program) to produce electronic systems and goods ranging from high-definition television to robots to computer chips. EUREKA encourages high-tech firms, now numbering more than 1,600, to pool their projects and resources. In return, governments do their utmost to facilitate collaboration by giving priority to projects.

TELEMAN, another Community research program is designed to strengthen the scientific and engineering bases used for the design of

nuclear remote-handling equipment. It addresses basic problems associated with remote operation using computer-assisted teleoperators with
increasing degrees of autonomy, questions relating to teleoperation in
nuclear environments, and the integration of disciplines that make up
robotics.

The Telecommunications Complex

Worldwide, R & D spending on information technologies has risen from
$35 billion annually in 1986, and is projected to be $90 billion by the early
1990s. At that time, the electronic equipment industry will overtake the
automobile sector. The burgeoning telecommunications phenomena will
expand to 7 percent of the E.C.'s economy by the end of the century
from its present 2 percent. No single E.C. country accounts for more than
6 percent of the world's telecommunications market, whereas the United
States represents 35 percent. Yet, taken as a whole, the E.C. has a 20
percent world market. Since 1983 these 12 member states have built up
a European telecommunications policy all of which evolved from its 1987
Green Paper dealing with telecommunications services and equipment.
Mergers have helped clear the path for dominance. Sweden's Asea and
Switzerland's Brown Boveri recently united into a $17.8 billion electronic
goliath. Compagnie Generale d'Electricite of France acquired ITT's telecommunications equipment activities and now ties with AT&T for world
leadership in telecommunications services.

RACE, standing for Research and Development in Advance Communications in Europe, was created to encourage a favorable environment
for the development of telecommunications. The Community established
this program in 1986 as part of an overall strategy to promote the rational
development of the various telecommunication systems and services that
are emerging in Europe. With $580 million provided until June 1992, its
specific objective is to allow the gradual evolution toward a community
integrated broadband communications system.

STAR, the Special Telecommunications Action for Regional Development was launched in 1987 and aims to eliminate disparities in present
and future infrastructures. The management of the differentiation of services is the main challenge facing telecommunication administrations and
decision makers worldwide.

And the list goes on. Illustrated above is the considerable time, effort,
and expense being made by the European Community to assert itself as
the premier leader in science and technology, with future applications in
business to follow, all befitting the slogan "Europe for Europeans."

January 1, 1993, may not see the sun rise in sparkling fashion. More time
will be needed, but the season is upon us when Europe flexes its time for
muscle of recognition and independence. The year 1992 was targeted as a

time for Europe for Europeans, but the reality demands tradeoffs—some-one gains, others lose. Should the domino theory apply, conflicts between industrial nations will abound. Europe is on its way to becoming the world's single richest market. The New Europe is primarily the product of a continent-wide economic deregulatory movement where hundreds of rules that should have been discarded long ago are finally being swept away.

With one currency and one passport, E.C. wheels will soon roll across the continent unhampered by frontier barriers. Will those same wheels roll across the plains of America to claim victory? The U.S. can ill afford to lose its lead in scientific and technological innovation. Europe has gathered its best to drive us down the slide. The brain drain no longer survives as those skilled Europeans who were transplanted to American shores are returning to their native lands to head up programs of com-petitiveness. Will the E.C.'s gains be at the expense of American losses? Will the post-World War II infusion of U.S. funding to rehabilitate a devastated European oasis return to haunt us 50 years later?

THE EUROPEAN FREE TRADE ASSOCIATION

A supplement to the E.C.'s potential, with its 340 million people in 12 countries, will be the added strength of nations within the European Free Trade Association (EFTA) which was created in 1959 under the Stock-holm Treaty and founded in 1960. It is based in Geneva, Switzerland. As a counter-institution to the European Community, it became a major force in Europe. EFTA is a grouping of six European nations that are not presently members of the E.C. Several have applied for membership in the European Community. These nations trade freely among themselves, and each has a bilateral free trade agreement with the E.C. that allows it to export industrial goods (but not agricultural products) to the E.C. duty-free. Unlike the E.C., which has a common external tariff, EFTA mem-bers determine tariff levels independently vis-à-vis non-members.

Its three goals are: to achieve free trade in industrial items among the member nations; to assist in the creation of a single market embracing the nations of Western Europe; and to contribute to the expansion of world trade in general.

EFTA members are Austria, Finland, Iceland, Norway, Sweden, and Switzerland. (Liechtenstein is also a member through a special protocol resulting from its customs union with Switzerland.) Some of its former members are now members of the E.C. EFTA has a $640 billion economy compared to the E.C.'s $3.8 trillion economy.

Effective January 1, 1984, the last of the industrial trade barriers be-tween the E.C. and the members of EFTA were abolished. It marked the culmination of a series of free trade agreements signed by the E.C. and the individual EFTA countries in the early 1970s. Initially, these agreements eliminated import quotas on industrial products traded among E.C. and EFTA nations. Import duties on the bulk of these products were eliminated by 1977. For a second group of industrial products—mainly textiles and nonferrous metals—tariffs were phased out gradually over a longer period.

There is no common customs tariff within EFTA. Members impose their own rates of duty on products entering from outside the EFTA areas. Trade between EFTA and the European Community in 1988 represented 24.5 percent of all E.C. trade (a little more than E.C.-U.S. trade) and between 40 and 64 percent of EFTA's imports and exports. The value of E.C. trade with EFTA in 1988 was $220 billion, $56 billion more than trade between the E.C. and the United States.

In March 1989, EFTA agreed to open negotiations with the E.C. for a special and improved trading relationship, "to strengthen links between the trading groups ahead of the 1992 market unification." By year's end the European Community, meeting in Strasbourg, reached a broad agreement to create an enlarged free-trade zone that would include the six members of EFTA. On October 22, 1991 the E.C. and EFTA concluded their negotiations and agreed to form a new common market—the European Economic Area—thus forming a different economic rivalry and competition for the world. The 31 million people from EFTA nations with a per-capita income of $19,000 per year (twice that of the E.C. average) will add further resources in Europe's global struggle for market dominance. Once approved by the parliaments of the participating 19 countries, the Economic Area will have increased in geographic size by more than 50 percent, becoming the world's largest free-trade area, with more than 370 million consumers and 46 percent of world trade.

Also, in late 1989, EFTA officials in Geneva stated that Hungary, Poland, Yugoslavia, and the then Soviet Union had contacted them about the possibility of joining, with Hungary probably being the first to reach an agreement. (Membership in EFTA may become the stopping point for the remaining European countries prior to formal application to join the European Community.)

By the end of 1990, Austria and Sweden had formally applied for admission to the European Community, further indicating an ultimate uniting of continental nations into a colossus of people, power, and economic grasp.

THE CENTRAL EUROPEAN NATIONS

Until separation from the former Soviet bloc, Central Europe was referred to as Eastern Europe, but the preferred shift in title is part of a public relations attempt to further unite Europe into a pre-World War I collection of powerful states. At the same time, it leaves the descriptive name of Eastern Europe to include the former Soviet Union.

In the strictest sense, this earlier definition included five nations (East Germany, Czechoslovakia, Hungary, Poland, and Yugoslavia) with an estimated $425 billion economy, but in the broader meaning now excludes East Germany which united with West Germany and encompasses Romania (Rumania) and Bulgaria. (Albania presently remains removed from this recent shift toward western democracy.)

By January 1991, Central Europe accounted for only seven percent of the E.C.'s total trade, but this will certainly change dramatically. A major problem was the fact that no Central European nation had a convertible currency. Events of the fall of 1989 will lead to significant changes in her relationship to the E.C. and to the rest of the Western economies of Europe.

Thus far, the E.C. has proposed a plan to aid these nations to include: easier access to Western markets by lowering tariffs, especially for farm exports; direct gifts of farm machinery and pesticides to help Polish and Hungarian agriculture; more foreign investment in these two countries, encouraged by $1.1 billion in loans from the European Investment Bank over three years; professional and management training to give Poland and Hungary the skills to run a market economy; and environmental protection to help them clean up areas poisoned by years of over-industrialization and bad management.

In 1989, Central European nations' share of trade with E.C. countries was:

Imports—Poland, 14 percent; Rumania, 9 percent; Czechoslovakia, 9 percent; Hungary, 9 percent; Bulgaria, 0.2 percent; and Albania, 0.3 percent.

Exports—Poland, 13 percent; Rumania, 3 percent; Czechoslovakia, 10 percent; Hungary, 11 percent; Bulgaria, 7 percent; and Albania, 0.3 percent.

THE OLD EUROPE AS A NEW AND MORE POWERFUL EUROPE

In a few years, a united force will emerge. The New Europe is now composed of 23 Eastern and Western European nations with a population of 520 million and a gross national product of nearly $5 trillion, compared to the $4 trillion economy of the United States and Japan's $2 trillion.

In addition, a resourceful and integrated former Soviet common market of the future, with its millions of producers and eager consumers, can only enhance the strength of the new evolving Europe. (Some specialists argue differently since the present Commonwealth of Independent States is just across the Bering Strait from Alaska and therefore as a very close U.S.

neighbor, she could someday become part of our North American Community.)

Not long ago, many experts were writing Europe off. Now, many wonder what lies ahead for the Americas, in particular, the United States. Only if the leadership in Washington responds with ingenuity, speed, and resources can we tackle this thorny issue. Unless our government, in cooperation with industry, a passionate citizenry, and other hemispheric nations, cries out for swift action U.S. achievements will someday be recorded in history books describing the wonders of our past. Then we may all say "what might have been!"

2

ACROSS THE PACIFIC

Japan and the East Asian Newly Industrialized Countries (EANIC) are on the move, preparing for what many Washington and Tokyo experts believe will be a final test of global determination at winning the war for trade dominance. The Asian area (composed of Japan, Hong Kong, Singapore, South Korea, and Taiwan) today represents that part of the world with the greatest growth potential. Six of the world's ten largest ports are still in Asia, together with the six largest banks. In the arena of trade balance, Japan's surplus jumped from $12.1 billion in 1980 to more than $60 billion in less than 10 years.

The transition for the Pacific Rim nations is astounding. In 1965, these countries produced a total of $183 billion in goods and services, just over one third of Europe's production and only one quarter of North America's output. By 1983, their explosive growth had increased total production eightfold to $1.7 trillion, fully one-half of North America's production and more than two-thirds of Western Europe's output. By the beginning of the 1990s, the combined gross national product of the region equaled that of Europe, and was three-quarters the total for North America. (It is projected, at this pace, the Asian Pacific nations' economies will account for 25 percent of the world's production by the beginning of the new millennium, compared with less than 30 percent for North America.)

By the spring of 1991, Americans began to see a turnaround in their trade relations with Japan. When the U.S. bilateral deficit with Japan peaked in 1987, at $57 billion, American exports to Japan had grown by 72.3 percent—from $28.2 billion to $48.6 billion. In 1990, U.S. exports to Japan increased by 9.2 percent; imports from Japan fell by 4.2 percent. The overall trade deficit with Japan had fallen by 16.2 percent, continuing the downward trend in the U.S.-Japan trade imbalance.

In fact, the U.S. deficit with Japan, which amounted to $38 billion in 1990, was at its lowest level since 1984. This trend was made possible not only by the yen's appreciation but by a series of conspicuous efforts on Japan's part to deregulate, to reform the economic structure, and to change the economy from an export-pulling one to a domestic demand-pulling one. Moreover, substantial import-promotion measures, including tax incentives, had been introduced by 1990.

By 1991, U.S. exports to Japan had increased 12 times ($28.2 billion to $48.6 billion) as much as Japan's exports to the U.S. ($88 billion to $89.7 billion) since 1987. In 1990, U.S. exports increased by $4.1 billion. Japanese exports to the U.S. fell by $3.9 billion in 1990, the first time they had fallen since 1975.

On the other side of the ocean, Japan has been both active and creative. Japan invested more than $30 billion in the European Community in 1989. European Community exports to Japan were $20 billion, with imports at $48.4 billion, thus producing a deficit of more than $26 billion.

Many Japanese executives view acquisitions as faster and cheaper routes to becoming European insiders than building factories. The trend began in earnest in 1988 when Japanese banks and firms began investing, buying real estate, buying European firms, setting up manufacturing subsidiaries, and boosting sales forces all over the European Community.

As most internal trade barriers fall by the end of 1992, the European Community becomes a prime target for Japanese goods. Japanese executives worry that 1992 will mean an insecure Europe, one beholden politically to home companies and the jobs they provide, frightened and determined to resist Japanese competition. As everyone knows, 1992 has not been designed to the benefit of outsiders.

Equally important, Asian dependence on the U.S. market continues to fade. Intra-Asian exports today make up over 40 percent of the total external trade of Asians. By the end of this century trade among Asian states could reach 55 percent. Its regional trade is growing at twice the pace of trade with North America, and four times more than Asian trade with Europe.

United States exports to EANIC and Japan in 1989 were $72.5 billion, while U.S. imports from these nations reached $153.0 billion, producing a U.S. deficit of $80 billion.

CAPITAL RICH JAPAN

It is investment that drives this rapid expansion of Asian trade. The 1980s saw an enormous surge of capital shift into the region, with Japan a principal source. Japanese investment has grown on average 50 percent per year in all of the four newly industrial economies (EANIAC). Yen flow into the ASEAN (Association of South East Asian Nations) 4—the largest ASEAN economies (Indonesia, Malaysia, the Philippines, and Thailand), have increased on average 100 percent per annum over the same period.

The cause and result of this capital infusion have been a shift of manufacturing capability from Japan to the rest of Asia. Concurrently there has been an immense technology transfer (valued at perhaps $1 billion) primarily linked to manufacturing. Immense percentages of the global production of many Japanese manufactured goods actually flow from other Asian nations.

Wherever you look, Japan is providing aid and/or investment. It announced a plan to offer a $1 billion economic aid package for Poland and Hungary ensuring its presence in Eastern Europe. From Eastern to Western Europe, Japan is seen everywhere. Suzuki Motor Company agreed to build a $140 million automobile factory in Hungary. Sony Corporation has been in Italy for more than 20 years producing audio cassettes. Matsushita, Japan's biggest electronic maker, started its 15th factory in Europe in 1990 with a highly automated plant making facsimile machines.

Japan's impressive foreign direct investment as of March 31, 1990 was $253,896 million. This excludes its overseas real estate transactions since September 1980. Worldwide investment in the manufacturing sector totalled $66,127 million and $182,516 million in the nonmanufacturing sector. Branch offices totalled $4,659 million and real estate transactions $595 million.

Trade skirmishes will not deter most Japanese executives. Indeed, E.C. internal integration is accelerating a strategic shift for Japan's major firms: a move away from exports and toward becoming insiders in major global markets, with substantial investments throughout the European Community. The Japanese know a basic economic principle, which they are practicing very well, that the economies of scale provided by a larger market make the risks easier to bear.

Cultural and language barriers throughout have been an obstacle for the Japanese when scouring Europe for plant investments. When they first began to invest on the Continent, the first priority was England, because of the language attraction. The Japanese wanted their overseas workers to learn English. Between 1971 and 1986, 50 Japanese plants opened in Britain. Between 1987 and 1989, 50 more had been established. Japan invested in Germany because their people are similar—punctual and rigid. France was third, because the government is strong politically in the European Community.

But now, Japanese investors and corporate strategists go anywhere the business climate is a sound match for them. Nissan, for example, opened a centralized European headquarters in Amsterdam. Therefore, as far as

1992 regulations are concerned, the Japanese are convinced it would be considered a European company, much the way Ford and Sony are. (Sony opened its first European factory in the early 1960s, thus becoming a part of the economic fabric of Europe.)

Since 1989 Japanese firms have invested more than $10 billion in the five leading economies in Southeast Asia, and more than $2 billion in Taiwan and South Korea. Although Japan's investment in the region remains less than one-fifth of its total investment abroad, East Asia's share of the total has grown more than eightfold over the past 10 years. By the year 2000, the combined population of the most promising markets in East Asia will be more than 600 million, nearly double that of the European Community.

When the U.S. government decided to make the U.S. dollar cheaper in 1985, it drove the Japanese overseas to remain competitive. For example, in 1980 American investment in Thailand was double that of Japan. Ten years later, Japan accounted for 50 percent of total foreign investment in Thailand, while the U.S. share was just 14 percent. The Japanese Ministry of Finance indicates that the nation's direct foreign investment in Asia for the first half of 1990 was in billions of yens: Indonesia—59, Hong Kong—144, Singapore—49, South Korea—19, China—24, Thailand—77, Malaysia—50, and the Philippines—12.

EANIC AND CHINA

If Japanese investment began the boom in intra-regional trade, it is the EANICs, especially Taiwan and Hong Kong that have propelled it. Taiwan's external Asian investments were only $60 million dollars as recently as 1986. The 1990 figure of $3.2 billion is a 53-fold increase.

Despite its more than $25 billion exports a year, the E.C.'s trade with Japan exceeds $30 billion as imports pass a staggering $55 billion. The volume of E.C.-Asian imports and exports (including Japan) reached more than $70 billion in 1990—a 10 percent increase over 1987 levels. Imports to the E.C. constitute two-thirds of that figure, resulting in significant trade deficits.

Southern China may win the fight to be the fifth East Asian Newly Industrialized Country. South China's Guangdong province, Hong Kong, Macau, and the global Cantonese ethnic diaspora, are joining economically to create what the Hong Kong-U.S. Chamber of Commerce has named the Cantonese economy—65 million people with a gross domestic product (GDP) of $80 billion in 1988.

Part of this international framework eventually makes its way onto the balance sheets of Beijing. Though still lagging behind the rest of the region, China's GNP nonetheless increased 150 percent during the period 1979–1988. Total Chinese trade with the Asian-Pacific region reached $48 billion in 1987, and $68 billion in 1989—a 42 percent increase in two years, and 60.7 percent of total Chinese external trade.

The stated intention of the government is to further open the economy. Foreign investment is to be the engine driving a doubling of GNP by the end of the century.

By early 1991 China's growing trade surplus with the United States was only surpassed by Japan. China's surplus was about $11 billion in 1990 as Americans claimed that the Chinese were dumping products or selling them at below cost, and were circumventing U.S. import quotas by shipping goods through other nations. The issue is whether to strip China of commercial privileges and raise tariffs on billions of dollars of toys, apparel, and other Chinese exports in the U.S. Chinese textiles represent one-fifth of its U.S. surplus, and China manufactures about half the toys imported by the United States. This swelling surplus is bound to increase the irritation of relations between the U.S. and China.

European Community-Chinese trade has risen fourfold since 1978, when it stood at $3 billion.

SELF-FUNDING ASIA

The intra-Asian investment flows which move from Japan and the wealthier Newly Industrializing Economies (NIEs) to other parts of the region are part of an emerging regional pattern of capital flow that is significantly different from that of the past. With the U.S. mired in its budget deficits and Western Europe increasingly drawn toward investment in the revitalization of Eastern Europe and in its preparation for post 1992 of the European Community, Asia must anticipate a need to be financially self-reliant.

The money to achieve this is already present in Asia. With NIE savings rates as high as 35 percent, a Japanese surplus of $80 billion, Japanese external assets of $400 billion, and Taiwanese reserves of $70 billion, Japan and the NIEs have the resources to be bankers not only to Asia, but to the entire world.

JAPAN-ASIAN ECONOMIC RELATIONS

In a cultural context, Japan's relations with the world suggest that it must establish a more balanced relationship with its Asian neighbors. Achievement of this goal will require not only continued industrialization of the region, but also the shedding of attitudes left over from the era of foreign domination. Dr. Kobayashi, Dean and Professor of Business at Keio University and Director of Mazda Motor Corporation, claims that "Japan believes that the Asia-Pacific region has the potential to become a locomotive for the world economy in the 21st century. But the economy in the driver's seat of the regional economy must be younger than Japan's" is today. Japan's role will be as a source of capital, especially as the funder of government borrowings within the region.

BEFORE THE PACIFIC CENTURY—THE 1990s

While Asia has the financial, technological, and human resources to be a self-sustaining regional economy, its development could be set back by uncontrollable factors in the global economic, political, and security environment. Conflicts worldwide will abound dealing with blocism, values, protectionism, latent nationalism, bio-environmental concerns, etc. Asia will certainly have its problems in the decade ahead, but its difficulties will be small compared to those of Europe, where a danger of all-out systematic collapse remains a possibility.

If Asia is personified as the "little dragon," European nations should be depicted as "dancing dinosaurs." Foreign, especially American, investors may soon discover that a dollar's worth of hope invested in Central Europe tomorrow will never pay the returns that a dollar's worth of actual opportunity invested in East Asia can pay today," according to Steven Scholosstein, author of *Trade War* and *The End of the American Century*.

With its envied U.S. trade deficit of more than $80 billion and E.C. trade deficit of $28 billion, Japan can lean heavily on her neighboring nations to relieve her of excess capacity and any inability to compete with lower wages and mass inputs of production hours. Should this self-fulfilling prophecy lead to increased American investment in Asia at the expense of Europe and nations within the American hemisphere then the prediction of Asian economic superiority moves one step closer to reality.

By the beginning of 1991 Japan's economy started to slide, where the second-longest expansion in her post-World War II history began to slow down. A combination of factors, high interest rates, a stock market crash, the plunging yen, the fading of property investments, and uncertainty in the Middle East, were greatly responsible for her declining expansion. But by all accounts, this will be temporary.

Relations between Tokyo and Washington are strained. Including all forms of investment, Japan is soon to overtake Britain as the number one foreign investor in America, this accompanied by charges that lavish Japanese spending on lobbying, think tanks, and research is an attempt to shape U.S. decision-making. Japan's trade surplus grew by 24 percent to $8.7 billion in April 1991, its highest level for two years. An expected continuation of this trend will certainly sour future trade relations.

Making the atmosphere even colder was the U.S. disappointment at Japan's stance in the 1990 Uruguay Round of the GATT talks. After being apparently indifferent at the outset, Japan was the first to reject a last-minute compromise on agriculture, with GATT talks collapsing soon after. That dismay, spilling over into U.S.-Japan relations, will damage long-term arrangements. While America's overall trade deficit is narrowing, the gap with Japan, stuck at around $50 billion since the late 1980s, may have nowhere to go but up, primarily because of the cheaper yen, making Japanese goods less expensive for overseas buyers.

Further progress is still required in the so-called Structural Impediments Initiative that is designed to change ingrained Japanese distribution and procurement practices which U.S. exporters feel shut them out of the market.

The problem is that the Japanese do not freely allow the competitive marketing of American products in Japan. Trade tensions with the U.S. continue over everything from semiconductors and mini-vans to agricultural products. Japan continues to allow foreign rice to be imported, although this is expected to change where at least 3 percent of the domestic rice market will soon be brought in from overseas. Some two decades of unfair trade practice have brought on the $100 billion annual imbalance and helped in large part to create the U.S. budget deficit.

All is not lost. In a sudden reversal to avoid another important trade conflict, Japan acceded to a May 31, 1991 deadline to avoid U.S. sanctions and will allow foreign companies to bid on a variety of big construction jobs. In exchange, Washington abandoned sanctions against some of Japan's biggest construction companies.

A few days later, on June 3rd, 1991 negotiators of the two nations agreed to extend for at least three years a set of rules covering bilateral trade in computer chips. The agreement suspended a $155 million in U.S. sanctions against the Japanese and specified that the American share of the Japanese chip market would rise to 20 percent.

Automobiles are the flywheel of the trade machinery. America's trade deficit with Japan is four times that of its next deficit partner. Our largest deficit commodity with Japan is automotive products (four times larger than the next deficit commodity). The U.S. trade surplus with Japan for aerospace products (our most successful category) is about $2 billion; Japan's trade surplus with the U.S. for automotive products is $32 billion annually. Automobiles continue to be an irritant. On May 31, 1991 America's Big Three automakers accused Japanese makers of dumping mini-vans into the U.S. market at below the price for the same vehicles in Japan.

At the same time, the Japanese, for example, feel little warmth for the U.S. as a nation and for its population. Respondents blame U.S. firms for the limited success of their exports to Japan and believe America is trying to unfairly pressure Japan on trade issues. They believe America's increasing dependence on Japanese technology gives Japan more clout in its dealing with the U.S. Japanese public opinion overwhelmingly expects their nation to eventually replace America as the world's leading economic and political power.

Asia is well aware of its destiny as it places new factories throughout the globe ready to take on any artificial barriers to halt its onslaught.

A new lexicon shows the popular vernacular of the region to include the nickname "JapaNIEs," showing Japan's deepening relations with Asia's newly industrializing economies (NIEs). Most Japanese companies have transferred much of their production to Asia. Japan's trade with Asia grows at an astounding clip of 30 percent annually, with predictions that the two-way trade of $250 billion will surpass that between Japan and the U.S. in the early 1990s, making the region's economy the fastest growing in the world. By 1995 it is expected that an Asian Community, paralleling the European Community will exist with natural market integration free of a formal, institutional framework.

As the world's largest aid donor, Japan now hands out nearly $7 billion a year in Asia, with imports from the region rising by 68.6 percent from 1986 to 1988, compared with 31.5 percent for the U.S.

It was often said that "Japanese don't invent things, they just copy other people's ideas." Whether this was once true, it no longer remains so. Japan spent about $67.5 billion on R&D in the 1987–1988 fiscal year, 7 percent more than the year before. This was a record 2.8 percent of the nation's gross national product, 0.1 percentage point ahead of the U.S. More than a quarter of the developed globe's scientists are Japanese, more than those from Britain, Germany, France, and Italy put together.

According to the Ministry of International Trade and Industry (MITI), Japan spends 0.26 percent of its gross national product on basic research, nearly as much but not quite matching the United States.

Clearly, Japan's economic stretch across Asia continues. Trade between her regional neighbors—the so called "yen block"—soars. Intraregional trade grew from 33 percent of the region's total exports and imports in 1980 to 37 percent by the end of the decade. The share of world trade increased to 20 percent. Significantly, direct investment by Japan in the Asian nations rose from $2 billion in 1985 to a very impressive $8.2 billion in 1988.

In addition, by September 1991 Japan's increasing trade surplus hit a record high of $9.7 billion for nine consecutive months of expansion. The month's trade surplus with the United States, in just one year, jumped more than seven percent to $4.62 billion. Japan's export to the U.S. that same month rose 2.9 percent from the previous year, to $8.52 billion, while her imports dropped 1.8 percent, to $3.9 billion.

Some feel that Japan won't slow down long enough for others to adjust to her charging assault. Attempts to put a brake on her thrust appear weak. Whether it be "rules of content," "quotas," or "accusations of dumping" Japan and her EANIC companions have a determination to win the trade and economic conflicts, for they envision a new era where their time has come.

3

THE EUROPEAN COMMUNITY'S FOOTHOLD IN THE AMERICAS

While most of the industrialized world trades actively with Mexico, Central and South American nations, no long-term strategy to court and massage these countries has been matched by the effort of the European Community. Steadily, for more than twenty-five years, strong ties have been built with determination and confidence.

THE FIRST STEP IN THE AMERICAS

The European Community has not been asleep when it comes to Latin America. Development cooperation was provided for in the E.C.'s 1957 Treaty. However, as far as the western hemisphere it was initially restricted to a few Caribbean islands.

Then, the European Community established its first South American tie in 1961 with Brazil in a cooperation agreement on the peaceful uses of nuclear energy.

In November 1974, the Commission presented a communication on development aid pointing out the need to extend it to the non-associated countries, including those in the Americas. An allocation was made in the E.C. budget for the first time in 1976 and implementation began, on an experimental basis, with the dynamic support of the European Parliament.

The first generation of cooperation trade agreements with Latin America commenced at the end of the 1970s. They were outline agreements covering every possible aspect of cooperation, although they provided neither trade preferences nor specific financial means.

Financial and technical cooperation agreements over this same period between the European Community and the Americas totaled $92,555,725 in Central America and $42,160,305 in the Andean Pact nations (Bolivia, Colombia, Ecuador, Peru, and Venezuela). The Andean Pact has gradually set up efficient community institutions (interestingly enough, parallel to those in the European Community). They include the JUNAC (Junta del Acuerdo de Cartagena), which is the organ of technical and administrative integration, like the E.C. Commission, and is in an excellent position to channel the E.C.'s financial and technical cooperation to help the regional integration drive of its five members.

The European Community's presence in respect to the JUNAC is therefore appreciated. The E.C. is the Junta's main external funder and has made it possible to run major pre-investment programs in the development sphere in rural, industrial, and energy sectors. These schemes, which have an obvious snowballing effect as potential triggers of further action and intrusion into the economy, have made a significant contribution to the integration cause. In particular, they have improved the extent to which the JUNAC can prepare and propose measures to redirect the integration process, which have led to the adoption of the Protocolo Modificatorio de Quito to the Cartagena Agreement setting up the Andean Pact. Total aid to the Junta over this period was approximately $32 million, divided as follows: rural sector—42 percent, food—24 percent, food technology—8 percent, economic and industrial planning—24 percent, and energy—2 percent.

The Central American Common Market (CACM) (formed in 1960 with the parties to the Treaty being El Salvador, Guatemala, Honduras, and Nicaragua, with Costa Rica joining in 1962) also conveniently modeled after the European Community, began receiving E.C. support at the time it was in serious difficulty. Following a decade of expansion, these nations were undermined by the world recession which had cut their external export earnings dramatically and caused a financial crisis. And since this meant the balance of intra-regional transactions could not be paid, it in turn blocked trade and reduced industrial production, which had been built up in the light of the Common Market, to practically nothing.

The E.C.'s approach to financial and technical cooperation in this subregion had long been geared primarily to each of the member nations. Then, the signing of a non-preferential cooperation agreement between the European Community and Central America (including Panama and the five CACM nations) relieved the E.C.'s desire to cooperate to promote regional integration.

Annual trade between the E.C. and the nations of Central America (Costa Rica, Guatemala, Honduras, Nicaragua, Panama, and El Salvador) in the late 1980s was more than $14 million. More than 80 percent of Central American exports (in value) enter the E.C. duty-free or are subject to low tariffs. Bananas are duty-free in several member states. Coffee beans have a 4.5 percent preferential tariff.

THE JUNE 1987 STRATEGY

At its meeting in Luxembourg on June 22, 1987 the Council of the E.C. adopted a policy paper outlining an overall, coordinated strategy for strengthening relations between the E.C. and Latin America, following developments in the restoration of democratic systems in most Latin American nations.

The Council was also recognizing the additional historical and cultural dimension which the accession of Spain and Portugal to the E.C. brought to the traditional links between the two regions. It was affirming the community of values and interests between the peoples of Europe and Latin America and their shared aspiration toward a society based on the observance of human rights.

The strategy adopted by the Council for strengthening relations was based on three main courses of action: the intensification of political relations, proposed informal consultations on major international economic issues affecting the two regions, and more extensive economic and trade cooperation which would take into account Latin America's level of development and the individual nation's differing requirements.

Likewise, in June of 1987, when meeting in Madrid for the European Council six-month summit, the Heads of State called for "continued development of political contacts and of economic, technical, commercial and financial cooperation between the Community and Latin America."

The interest taken by the European Parliament in all the events in Latin America testified strongly to the community of values between the peoples of the two regions. Between July 1987 and July 1989, almost 63 resolutions were adopted on subjects concerning Latin America, and delegations from the E.C. Parliament paid a number of visits there. On August 22, 1988 a group of members of the European Parliament went to Esquipulas, the site of the future Central American Parliament, and there they confirmed the E.C.'s wish to contribute to the setting up of this Parliament.

Mindful of Latin America's struggling economy, the European Community and other nations are treading slowly in over-financing many of these governments. Despite its lack of formal powers in this sphere, the European Community began to play an increasingly active role in seeking solutions to the growing urgency created by the debt of "middle-income developing countries," a category that includes the Latin American nations. A proposal from Spain, a new member of the European Community, for setting up a "European Guarantee Fund" reducing heavily indebted countries' debt-servicing payments and the level of their external debt was placed before the E.C.'s Council.

The foothold by the European Community began with its formal representation in Latin America dating to 1965, the year its High Authority opened a "liaison office" in Santiago de Chile with the Latin American Iron and Steel Institute (ILAFA). In 1967, it became the Latin American Delegation of the Commission of the European Communities, and this was the only Community "base" in the entire region until 1978, when the Delegation was transferred from Santiago to Caracas, Venezuela, and the Santiago office became a branch of the Caracas Delegation. A number of other Commission Delegations have been opened over the years, increasing the E.C.'s ever-presence: Mexico, Costa Rica, Uruguay, Peru, Ecuador, and Brazil.

The Commission Delegations have the status of diplomatic missions. They maintain contact with the authorities and business people and economic groupings in the host nations, prepare and monitor development cooperation and economic cooperation with the host nations, and keep the Commission in Brussels regularly informed of events in the region. A Commission press and information service in Caracas with documentation centers in Caracas and Santiago is responsible for keeping interested parties and the Latin American public in general informed about the E.C. and its activities.

On the initiative of many leading figures in the two regions, the European Parliament, the E.C., the Latin America Interparliamentary Conference, and the Commission advocated the setting-up of an institute to promote and intensify relations between the European Community and Latin America. Since 1985, the Institute for European-Latin American Relations (IELAR), which is based in Madrid, has been conducting studies, holding conferences, and producing publications on economic and political problems of concern to both regions.

TRADE BETWEEN THE E.C. AND LATIN AMERICA

While the Community is still of major importance to Latin America as a trading partner (over 20 percent of its exports go to the E.C. and almost 20 percent of its imports come from the E.C.), Latin America has lost some of its importance as an E.C. market, at least for the present. The E.C.'s exports to the region account now for some 4 percent of its total trade, as compared with 6 percent in the early 1980s.

Almost all of the E.C.'s exports to Latin America are capital goods, which accounted for over half the total exports: agricultural and industrial machinery (20 percent), motor vehicles (10 percent), and electrical equipment (11 percent).

Conversely, E.C. imports from Latin America are mainly agricultural produce and foodstuffs (over 50 percent of the total), energy (some 15 percent), and ore and metal (15 percent). Primary products therefore account for almost 80 percent of Latin America's exports to the E.C. The structure of Latin American trade is consequently such that it is vulnerable to external factors such as fluctuations in commodity prices or reduced demand for certain products as a result of technological changes or changes in other nation's policies.

All is not running smoothly for the European Community in its trade relations with the southern hemisphere. In just a few years the shift away from the E.C. has become more dramatic as the Community has increased its imports of manufacturers from other world regions; and the structure of Latin American exports to the United States has become more diversified, with 21 percent capital goods and 18 percent consumer goods. Not only has the E.C. failed to adapt to demand within the markets, but trade between the two regions shows a large degree of geographical concentration. Almost two-thirds of this trade is conducted with three E.C. states—Germany (30 percent), France, and Italy.

The European Community has several strategies in place for improving trade with Latin America. The Community has been granting Latin American nations autonomous, non-reciprocal tariff benefits. All manufacturers and some 400 agricultural products are covered by the Community scheme of preference. For these products, the customs duties are cancelled, or more often reduced. Some $27 billion worth of E.C. imports therefore come in at a zero or reduced rate of duty, so that the E.C. relinquishes customs revenue of more than $1 billion.

In addition, the E.C. has worked out a number of measures for making exports from Latin America more attractive. In 1987 customs duties on unroasted coffee, cut flowers, and tobacco were lowered. Similarly, the restructuring of the scheme for industrial products in 1986 and textiles in 1988 resulted in a reduction in the number of quantitative limits and the differentiation which this brought about has greatly improved the opportunities for preferential access.

THE MAKINGS OF A CLASH

There remains an increasing reciprocal interest and political link between the E.C. and the Latin American hemisphere. The European Community plans to play a more active part in seeking solutions to the debt problem of Latin America. Through its different industrial cooperation instruments, it can further the Latin American countries' efforts to modernize their industrial structures and diversify their exports. It can enlist Latin American scientists and engineers in its own efforts to be in the vanguard of scientific and technological progress. It can give the Latin American nations the benefit of its political experience as regards economic integration.

The E.C.'s progress toward the single market and European union is increasing its political responsibilities and providing it with resources for taking action in relation to the rest of the world. In view of its traditional links with Latin America, it is bound to pursue a rapprochement with this region, which has considerable political and economic potential.

The European Community's strategy toward Latin America ties in with Europe's own interests. They both overlap. The E.C. Commission, prodded by the Bush Administration, has decided to double its aid to Central America (currently at $120 million annually) between 1991 and 1993. The Europeans are also being asked to contribute $100 million to an investment fund that is part of Bush's Latin American plan.

On the commercial front, European firms have been important players in buying up newly privatized Latin American firms. Spain's Iberia Airlines, for example, has purchased a majority stake in Aerolineas Argentinas, the formerly state-run national carrier of Argentina, while France's Telecom and the Italian company STET have taken over one of Argentina's two privatized telephone systems. For firms of E.C. nations, the scheduled free-trade zone between Argentina, Brazil, Uruguay, and Paraguay is a future magnet for investment.

This might be considered a criss-cross burden sharing. While the U.S., despite its self-proclaimed financial constraints, is being urged to remain active in Eastern Europe, the European Community states are sought after in Mexico and Latin America. A compelling force for France, Italy, Spain, and Portugal of any aid or investment effort in the southern hemisphere is their cultural affinity with the region, thus giving them a greater case to influence, as contrasted with a smaller opportunity in Eastern Europe. To press for their continuing foothold in the Americas, the E.C. signed a cooperation accord with Mexico in April 1991 in hopes of increasing mutual trade. The agreement is similar to the one the Community signed earlier with Argentina and Chile.

In July, 1991, nations in the Americas that were once colonies of Spain and Portugal, the countries of Ibero-America, met in Guadalajara, Mexico. The presidents of 19 Latin American nations and the rulers of Spain and Portugal agreed to meet each year, further cementing their cultural, linguistic, and economic dependence across the Atlantic.

At the same time I met with Mr. Antonio Cunha Vaz, of the Portugal E.C. delegation (Bureau of Information) in Lisbon and learned that Spain was rapidly acquiring Portuguese firms as well as other companies in South America, thus further solidifying the grip of the European Community in the western hemisphere.

Presently, direct investment in Latin America is dominated by the United States, for example, U.S. firms account for 61 percent of all foreign direct investment in Mexico. However, there are indications of change.

With the emerging influence of Spain and Portugal, the E.C. will turn greater attention and funding to Latin America. It is instinctively appropriate in this period of searching for markets that German and other more northern E.C. states stress opportunities to their east. Convincingly, Spain and Portugal are natural links to Central and South America.

The campaign goes on for the hearts, minds, and resources of the Latin American regions. As these nations struggle to pull themselves away from debt and poverty, the European Community will properly attempt to take advantage of their richer position, with both a lengthy historical involvement with the zone, and with the funds from across the ocean. Deals made between the E.C. and countries in the southern hemisphere continue to expand, making it all the more difficult for the nations of the northern hemisphere to counter. Should the opportunity be lost, the New American Community will assuredly know the source of its predicament, and will search for an answer to why it waited so long for a unified response.

4

JAPAN'S STRATEGY IN LATIN AMERICA

ENTRENCHED IN MEXICO

Japan has been involved in the lands south of the United States since the early part of the twentieth century. The pace has quickened since then, as Japanese investment has focused in on a few of the Latin American nations, all for different reasons.

Now that global trade has become a reality, Japan is especially interested in a relationship with Mexico, in particular because of its proximity to the U.S. market. By the late 1980s, 77 of the 126 Japanese firms in Mexico worked in manufacturing. Nissan Motor Company employed close to 5,000 workers. In 1985 two major steelwork projects were completed with substantial Japanese investment. Sumitomo Metal Industries and another 51 Japanese companies invested U.S. $20 million, or 40 percent of the total, in the construction of a large diameter pipe plant and Kobe Steel and 51 other firms invested U.S. $22 million in constructing an industry of large-sized cast and forged steel products.

Just across the border from the United States, Nissan Mexicana invested $1 billion, $400 million of it in a new car factory in Aguascalientes. Most of the completed cars are to be shipped to Latin American nations, and in late 1992, back to Japan from Mexico.

Frictions remain. Japan's private sector, which accounts for less than 10 percent of Mexico's foreign investment is put off by Mexico's investment law. When the Japanese ambassador to Mexico called for a more profound change in the investment law, he was firmly renounced by the leftist Mexican press.

In addition, in the summer of 1990 a group of U.S. television manufacturers and labor unions complained to the U.S. Commerce Department that five Japanese (and two Korean) picture tube manufacturers were violating anti-dumping regulations on exports to the U.S.

This anti-dumping issue is likely to grow as part of the increasingly difficult debate over the role of the Japanese maquiladoras (so-called screwdriver assembly plants) in the U.S.-Mexico free-trade accord. For example, presently a number of Japanese maquiladoras export to the U.S. through the General System of Preferences (GSP), a program for encouraging trade from emerging countries under which items enter the U.S. duty-free if they have at least 35 percent Mexican value added.

With a U.S.-Mexican free-trade agreement, the GSP could be replaced by fairly tight regional content requirements, probably not less than 70 percent U.S. or Mexican content. This would become another way to guarantee that the free-trade accord would not become a backdoor to the United States. Japanese maquiladoras will face protectionist assaults from U.S. competitors. Political pressures will force U.S. and Mexican free-trade negotiators to require Japanese maquiladoras to use higher levels of North American content than the Japanese have expected.

For years, the maquiladora program was truly the best of all worlds for Japanese firms, attracting such giants as Sony and Sanyo Manufacturing. Labor in Mexico is cheap, and the Mexican government makes the maquiladora an exception to nationalistic restrictions on 100 percent foreign ownership and also offers duty-free importation on high-quality Japanese components. And by channeling exports north through Mexico, the Japanese take advantage of U.S. tariff breaks without further skewing Japan's lopsided trade balance with the U.S.

Japan, as should be expected, will find Mexico an increasingly attractive arena for direct investment and a springboard for its superbly orchestrated manufacturing and trade exploits. Perhaps, in the short run, many North Americans will be trying to find ways to keep Japan away from Mexico.

NETWORKING LATIN AMERICA

The Latin American network with Japan has as its nucleus Brazil. Today, more than one million inhabitants of Japanese origin live in South America, nearly all of them in Brazil, which claims to have the largest number of Japanese outside of Japan.

It was in 1908 when the first 781 Japanese walked off a migrant ship to reach for the riches promised by a wild and tropical land. Instead, they found themselves replacing recently freed slaves on plantations in the heartland of Brazil. Clearing jungles, suffering from disease but facing prospects of dishonor should they return home, they instead stayed on. Over the next forty years, more than one-quarter of a million new Japanese emigrants arrived from Japan.

Within decades, the Japanese of Brazil came to represent one of the more impressive success stories of Latin America. Most of their children and grandchildren—the nisei and sansei—of the earliest poor settlers now are the well-educated, successful citizens of their new home.

At the same time, they have led the way for Brazil to becoming Japan's principal trade and investment partner in Latin America. In São Paulo, the largest and richest of Brazil's cities, more than one-half of these Japanese live and work. They are executives, translators, and secretaries, and provide a significant support system for nearly 400 business firms that operate there with Japanese capital. With investments totaling close to $4 billion, these companies are the largest foreign investors in Brazil after the United States and Germany.

The presence of these successful Japanese immigrants has become the focal point for Japanese investment in Brazil and throughout Latin America. They facilitate communications and seek and sponsor much of the investment from Japan. While hundreds of nisei and sansei work for Japanese giants such as Sony, Mitsubishi, and Honda, many work for Brazilians.

Nisei farmers produce about 70 percent of all the vegetables and fruit sold to metropolitan São Paulo's 14 million people. The Japanese Cotia is an impressive cooperative with 15,500 members linking farms in 15 states throughout Brazil. Typically, it started in the 1920s when 83 immigrant potato farmers got together because they felt cheated by local middlemen. Today, Cotia runs 23 experimental stations, its own agricultural school and has become the Latin American region's most prosperous cooperative. Similar to other nisei farms, Cotia exports large volumes of soybeans, fresh fruit, coffee, tea, cacao, and cotton—with much of it going to Japan.

To a great extent, both this model and network have been effectively used by Japanese industry and government as a springboard for bringing investment to Latin American nations and to serve as a central nerve station for communicating and protecting Japanese interests in the Spanish and Portuguese speaking regions of the western hemisphere.

In contrast with other nations of the world, Latin American nations have received a small amount of foreign direct investment from Japan. For example, until March 31, 1990, Latin American investment by Japan was U.S. $36,855 millions contrasted to $253,896 U.S. million worldwide. (Overseas real estate transactions have been excluded from Japan's foreign investment data since September 1980.)

Of Japan's direct investment in the late 1980s, 45.5 percent was placed in the United States, 10.6 percent in Europe and 4.3 percent in Australia and New Zealand, which together with that undertaken in Canada, gave two-thirds of the total to developed nations. .

With developing nations, Japan's investment of 18.5 percent was directed to three tax shelters (Panama, Cayman Islands, Bahamas), 10.4 percent to Asian nations, while Latin America (excluding Panama) received US $532 million or 2.4 percent of the total. Clearly, Japan has favored developed nations for investment. In fact, direct investment for manufacturing in the late 1980s dropped in developing countries from approximately 30 percent to about 17 percent over a two year period.

These investments in the Latin American manufacturing sector until March 31, 1990 totaled U.S. $5,633 millions and U.S. $66,127 millions worldwide. In the Latin American nonmanufacturing sector, investments total U.S. $31,153 millions and U.S. $182,516 millions worldwide.

Among nonmanufacturing sectors, the Latin American transport sector accounts for a large relative share (77.4 percent of the world total). Japanese firms, seeking to reduce tax disbursements, take advantage of the tax shelter system existing in Panama to invest in maritime transportation. In a three year period during the mid–1980s, direct investment by Japan in Panama amounted to US $5.6 billion as compared to only US $1.4 billion in the rest of Latin America. In fact, until the later part of the decade, Panama had consistently been the second largest (after the United States) individual recipient of Japanese direct investment.

Just under 15 percent of Japan's worldwide foreign direct investment has been directed to Latin America. Even without Panama, the geographical distribution of Japanese investment in Latin America has been very unequal. Brazil received 64.4 percent of the total, Mexico 27.4 percent, and the remainder of the many Latin American nations only 8.2 percent.

Little deters Japan from continuing to forge ahead. In November 1989 a major event cemented the relationship between Latin America and Japan. Finance ministers and central bank governors from south of the border nations met in Nagoya, Japan to attract Japanese investment. A three-day symposium was held, sponsored by the Inter-American Development Bank and Japan's Export-Import Bank. The private sector bankers received promises from the Japanese government for financial support to several Latin and Caribbean nations. An agreement to provide all or part of a promised $2 billion-plus loan to Mexico over three years was signed, as other loans to Central and South American nations continue to be negotiated. Japan is well poised for the penetration of a rich, consuming market far from its shores, but ever-increasing in importance to its plans for the future. In fact, Japan's foreign direct investment projections in Latin America in thirty years actually exceeded those in Europe.

Presently, approximately 15 percent of all Japanese worldwide foreign direct investment goes to Latin America, just under Asia at 16 percent and Europe at 18 percent. And there are few indications that Japan plans to curtail the pace or the percentage of its overseas investments to Latin America. The region has been targeted as extremely fertile and promising.

If Latin America bears relatively little importance for Japanese investors, Japanese investments also account for a small share of foreign investment in Latin American nations. Even in Brazil, a country which enjoys priority attention from Japan, Japanese direct investment, with an average of 9.2 percent of the total between 1982 and 1985, places third after the United States (32.1 percent) and Germany (13.2 percent).

More notable in terms of volume and proportion is loan capital provided by private Japanese banks to Latin American nations. Estimates suggest that the exposure of Japanese banks in the case of large Latin American debtors is only second to that of the U.S. commercial banks. By 1986, the cumulative debt of Argentina, Brazil, Mexico, Chile, and Venezuela with Japanese banks reached US $28.6 billion.

Although Japanese machinery and equipment exports to Latin American nations include a high proportion of consumer goods (automobiles, motorcycles, audio and video equipment, and television sets), a substantial part of these exports are industrial machinery, sophisticated office equipment, etc., which contributes to the modernization of the region's productive structure. By 1986 Japanese machinery exports to the 19 Latin American nations totaled US $6.4 billion. In addition, although accounting for only 3.1 percent of Japan's official development assistance throughout the world, four Latin American nations (Mexico, Peru, Brazil, and Bolivia) figured among the 18 major beneficiaries.

In summary, Japanese exports to Latin American nations rose from US $6.6 billion by the end of 1979, to US $8.9 billion in 1980 and to US $10.5 billion in 1981. By 1986, Japanese exports were US $9.5 billion. The rise of oil prices and other raw materials caused Japanese imports from the region to grow from US $3 billion to US $6 billion between 1978 and 1981, with an average from 1981 to 1986 at US $6.5 billion.

What is clear is that today, Latin America represents a market of secondary importance for Japan with only 4.5 percent of total exports and 4.9 percent of total imports. With 4.5 percent, Latin America ranked sixth on the list of Japanese exporters' priorities: 38.5 percent goes to the U.S., 20 percent to Southeast Asia, 14.7 percent to the European Community, 4.7 percent to the People's Republic of China, and 4.7 percent to the Middle East. In Japanese imports, favored positions were occupied that same year by Southeast Asia (23.3 percent), the United States (23 percent), the Middle East (14.6 percent), and the European Community (11.1 percent), with Australia, China, and Latin America forming a group of secondary markets.

Further, Japan's trade with Latin America is concentrated in a few nations. Panama received 41 percent and Mexico and Brazil 26 percent of Japanese exports to the region. Fifty-eight percent of imports stem from Brazil and Mexico, and another 30 percent from Argentina, Chile, Peru, and Venezuela.

For its part, trade with Japan presently bears relatively little importance for the majority of Latin American nations. Exports to Japan exceed 10 percent of the total only in the cases of Nicaragua and Peru, and are under 5 percent in 12 of the 19 countries. While the relative weight of Japan in Latin American imports is slightly higher, it only surpasses 10 percent in the Dominican Republic, Ecuador, Panama, Colombia, and Costa Rica.

The Japanese-Latin American trade structure is typical of trade between a developed nation and a developing area. A total of 82 percent of Japanese exports to Latin America correspond to machinery (40 percent are ships for Panama); 10 percent to basic and various manufacturers; 5 percent to metals; and 3 percent to chemical products. Twenty-five percent of coffee (265,000 tons) imported by Japan came from Brazil and 39 percent more from 12 other countries of the region; with 23 percent, Brazil was the second supplier of iron ore and concentrates; 14 percent of copper ore was obtained from Chile, Peru, and Mexico; 18 percent of lead ore from Peru and Honduras; and 25 percent of zinc ore from Peru.

Japan imports a considerable proportion of some chemical, steel, and non-ferrous metal products from Latin America. However, in addition to the fact that this relatively high share in Japanese imports is accounted for by a limited number of Latin American nations (Brazil, Mexico, and to a lesser degree Peru, Chile, and Venezuela), these products belong to a group whose consumption in the Japanese economy is clearly declining.

The 1991 Gulf War once again showed how dependent Japan is on imported oil. Now, having learned her lesson the hard way, she will turn to Latin America, especially Mexico, for future needs. Japan hopes that oil from across the Pacific Ocean will be made available in great abundance on the open market, thus lowering, if not eliminating, the concern about resource security. It is a gift of increasing importance to Japan, one that it will pursue with vigor.

Despite the fact that Latin America has historically been a market of secondary importance for Japan, and that it is concentrated in a few countries, capital investment and trade by Japan in Latin American nations, even at this limited scale, will contribute to the development of the countries. With increased transfers of technology and golden opportunities on the horizon to reach a market twice that of Europe and the United States, Japan will press hard to secure a strong presence south of the U.S. border.

Japan has emerged since the late 1980s as one of the world's largest donors of aid to developing nations, as well as a major government-to-government lender. Japan budgeted foreign aid of $6.5 billion for fiscal year 1991. Even though most of the aid and loans are aimed at Asia, where

Japanese corporations are centering their investments, Latin America has been targeted as an area to receive increased assistance. Equally important, Japan and other nations of the Pacific Rim are edging in on regions that were previously considered the domain of the United States. By becoming a greater exporter and consumer of services, Japan and other Asian countries will draw ever closer to the position of the U.S., as reflected in multilateral negotiations with respect to the regulation of international trade in goods and services. While Japan continues to lead the scientific and technological revolution, Latin American nations will surely adopt its advanced technologies, certainly encouraging the cementing of the relationship.

5

SUBSIDY DISCRIMINATION AND UNFAIR PRACTICES

While our two most competitive allies anticipate a growing gap in relationships with Spanish or Portuguese speaking nations in the western hemisphere, one that they are well-equipped to exploit, what is to be an appropriate course of action for countries, in general within the New American Community, and specifically, within North America?

The obvious solution to an inevitable declining U.S. living standard (unless corrective action is taken) and a permanent loss of economic global leadership is to evolve a competitive cooperative within North America first, then later all of the Americas. The potential has always been there, but the desire and the barriers were part of our history. These restraints are quickly falling and should be encouraged to dissolve at a more heightened pace. Survival of our bountiful living is at stake and a unified North American economy is the first step.

The shape of "Made in North America" (the United States, Canada, and Mexico) with its 365 million people, GNP of nearly $6 trillion and total trade of $225 billion has the potential muscle for leading the way for continued prosperity.

Several major events have encouraged the leadership in Washington, industrialists and business leaders across America, academics and other responsible citizens to conclude that the United States no longer commands its economic muscle of a mere few years ago. Our trade with Europe in the mid-1980s totaled $132.6 billion, roughly one fifth of all U.S. trade, but the United States posted a $26 billion trade deficit. Considering that the U.S. had a $19 billion trade surplus at the beginning of

that decade, our declining trade balance with Europe has actually out-
paced our growing imbalance with Japan. The European Community's
share of U.S. exports has declined from 35 percent to 18 percent, and
the E.C. continues to secure many of our former markets around the
globe.

The year 1990 ended with an uneasiness accompanied by a growing
resentment in the industrialized and third-world nations regarding unfair
trade practices. With the failure of the General Agreement on Tariffs and
Trade meeting toward 1990's end (although they were placed on the corrective track again in March 1991) and the utilization of Section 301 of
the Omnibus Trade Act, nerves were tense as Fortress Europe vs. Fortress America inched closer to reality.

Throughout the year accusations were tossed about dealing with quantitative restrictions and import surveillance, customs barriers, Buy American Restrictions, and tariff reclassifications, to name just a few. As Sir
Roy Denman, the European Community's Ambassador to the U.S. in the
1980s, noted: "What one does oneself is fair trade, and what the other
fellow does is unfair."

The dramatic course of economic events, some by design of American
leadership, others structured by our trading partners have brought Asia,
Europe, and the United States to a tangle of tariffs, protectionism, new
treaties, and attempts to seek solutions. These include the December 1990
collapse of GATT meetings and the passage and implementation of Super
301.

GATT

Thanks to the General Agreement on Tariffs and Trade, world trade
expanded faster than global output after the end of World War II. With
GATT, tariffs worldwide have been cut from an average of 40 percent in
1947 to less than 5 percent today and consumers have reaped rich rewards
in the form of lower prices and better merchandise. GATT has been
remarkably successful and crucial to a strong world economy.

However, the near disintegration, in December 1990, of the General
Agreement on Tariffs and Trade (GATT), (resurrected in March 1991)
almost led to numerous trade war casualties, with the United States probably the least affected. The United States still continues to have a continuing advantage of approximately 35 percent over its leading trading
partners in the output of goods and services per capita.

While realizing the loss of manufacturing in this country down from 29
percent of gross national product in 1950 to 21 percent in 1980, to 22
percent in 1987, manufacturing is merely a major, but not critical measure
of U.S. overall economic performance. (For the U.S., exports account
for 75 percent of manufacturing growth and 12 percent of GNP in 1989.)

The rest of the economy is made up of the trade, transportation, financial, insurance, real estate and services sectors, as well as government services. It is America's superior efficiency in the remaining 80 percent of its economy that has yielded the higher standard of living in the United States.

The December 1990 failure of the GATT negotiations came at a particularly unfortunate moment. For the first time in the history of GATT, many developing countries—Mexico and Brazil, for example—were voluntarily trying to develop the competitiveness and efficiency of market economies and were moving away from state participation and guidance. Central Europe was running away from managed trade. These nations must be allowed the opportunity to realize their comparative advantage in sectors such as agriculture and textiles. The best way to do this—far better than aid—is to give them access to markets. The GATT failure was a tragedy of exaggerated expectations. A tug of war primarily between the U.S. and the E.C. set the stage for eventual collapse. The world recorded in December 1990 that it was being plunged into trade wars and recession because of a European addiction to subsidizing farmers, which the U.S. fought with tooth and nail.

Should a trade war have broken out, these nations, as well as Japan and Europe, would have been vulnerable. The U.S. is much less so. The U.S., starting from a considerably higher position, is by far the largest, most homogeneous market in the world. Trade war is in nobody's interest, and the U.S. would lose significantly from it. But the U.S. market is more important to its trading partners than any one of their markets is to the U.S. The direct implication was that Japan and Europe stood to lose more from the December 1990 GATT failure than their policy makers seemed to realize.

For many U.S. experts the response to a collapsed December 1990 GATT meeting was "it's about time." The 43-year old framework for world trade appeared to have become obsolete. Evidence shows that GATT agreements do not necessarily boost U.S. economic growth, or narrow trade deficits significantly. Until there is assurance that all members of GATT contribute fully to the system and play by the same rules, pressure will continue to discard GATT principles and turn toward renewed protectionism, closing out foreign competitors.

Within days of the suspended talks in Brussels, the U.S. and several of its trading partners began saber rattling. The U.S. immediately started to prepare to raise duties on European exports of food and beverages by 200 percent, in part to retaliate against a European ban on pork and beef imports from the U.S. All sides must give, but the Europeans must give the most. In addition, the U.S. will long remember Japan's considerable role during the last days of the GATT sessions. The logjam, led by the E.C., demands a phasing out of most export subsidies.

A resurrected GATT round, with a timely signed agreement, will not diminish the significance of the tensions, or lessen the memories of the December 1990 collapse. While the U.S. argues that the European Community has five times more farmers than the United States, with only a slightly larger population to feed, it is absurd that governments artificially support these inefficient and not very profitable suppliers. The Uruguay Round of GATT may indeed find a future, but the frictions will long remain.

Farm and other agricultural subsidies may well be lowered in Europe, but political pressures will mount as farmers in the European Community take to the cities in protest of their threatened and overly protected livelihood. Europeans themselves will eventually force the resolution with a dramatic dismounting of the E.C.'s Common Agricultural Policy. Under CAP subsidy regulations 325 million Europeans pay twice for the E.C.'s farm inequity: as consumers and as taxpayers. Consumers pay inflated food prices because their market is insulated by levies from lower-priced imports. Taxpayers pay the subsidies needed to dump overpriced E.C. surpluses abroad.

Two months after the calamity of December 1990, the GATT meetings were to begin again. A crucial breakthrough on trade had surfaced. The E.C. agreed to demands from the U.S. and third world food exporters to negotiate specific reductions in each of three farm subsidies, thus opening the way for a bold trade agreement that could add trillions of dollars to the world's economies. The key turning point was the inclusion of agricultural trade as a part of GATT, thereby forcing subsidies to drop significantly. It would mark an end to the E.C.'s longstanding commitment to protect a few million family farmers. Prices were kept artificially high, stimulating production. The surplus stocks were then dumped onto foreign markets at subsidized prices, devastating farmers in developing nations. The policy cost European taxpayers $100 billion a year, perhaps the primary reason for the E.C.'s change of heart in the negotiations.

The 1990s and probably the next century will see the growth of bilateral trade agreements or regional blocs, i.e., the European Community, the New American Community. This doesn't mean an inevitable collapse or fragmentation of the world's trading system into these entrails. Instead, such free-trade agreements will be compatible with GATT principles. Columbia University Professor Jagdish Bhagwaiti suggests in his book *The World Trading System at Risk*, that "... Article XXIV (of GATT) be modified to make sure that any country joining a free-trade area reduce its tariffs to all GATT members." This way, free-trade areas can become "building blocks of, rather than stumbling blocks to, GATT-wide free trade."

Now that the breakthrough that paralyzed international trade has occured, negotiations must be tolerated every four years. GATT, at best, represents the turntable indicating that trade tensions abound throughout the world. Tradeoffs are ever present. You win and you lose at the same time. Free-trade accords among the countries of the New American Community, as bumpy and testy as they may appear, will more likely be threatened from outside. Looking down its Atlantic and Pacific coastal waters, the NAC will have its work cut out to protect its collective trade interests.

SUPER 301

Although the United States is in general terms a comparatively open economy, the European Community believes that it nevertheless maintains numerous unfair or discriminatory practices and legislative provisions which impede and distort trade and which undermine the multilateral trade regime itself. It demonstrated that, contrary to popular belief in the U.S., the U.S. is not free of the types of trade barriers condemned in an E.C. *National Trade Estimate Report on Foreign Trade Barriers.*

It would be incorrect to ascribe all the barriers and unfair practices of the United States as a clear indication of growing protectionism alone. This is undoubtedly the case to some extent, as a certain temptation to protect the U.S. domestic market is created by the persistent current account deficit, and it is certainly true of those elements of U.S. trade legislation which are incompatible with the multilateral obligations of the United States, e.g., mandatory, unilateral action under Section 301.

Other factors can be identified which lead to the types of measures described. For example, a piece of legislation which has been adopted for valid domestic reasons can have an unintended negative impact on the trade rights and opportunities of third nations. Thus, in general, divergent systems of economic regulation in different nations can give rise to problems between them. It is normal to solve such problems through bilateral consultation, with reference to international rules and using multilateral procedures where these are relevant.

However, such restrictive practices of unfair trade can raise doubts whether the United States is sufficiently committed to the multilateral system which provides the main reference point for resolving disputes. This is suggested not only by the adoption of numerous elements of trade legislation that conflict with multilateral rules, but also by the taking of clearly illegal measures, by the inordinate time taken to bring U.S. legislation into conformity with the ruling of trade panels, and by the inadequate U.S. participation in international rule-making.

The European Community, for example, is concerned by the extent to which non-tariff barriers to its exports now seem to be more and more at the state rather than at the federal level. In the U.S., an increasing proportion of procurement is at the state level, while state regulations on taxation, on financial and professional services, in the area of standards, etc., create serious handicaps to doing business in the U.S. market. Indeed, it is becoming clear that one of the major difficulties of selling into the U.S. market is the extent to which the market is heterogeneous and fragmented. Many nations believe that it is indispensable for the U.S. to eliminate the unilateral elements of its legislation and bring it fully into conformity with multilaterally agreed rules.

U.S. trade policy is marked by quotas and preferential rules, often the result of diverse political pressures. The U.S. still views such actions as necessary evils rather than parts of a coherent strategy to secure stability and growth. Section 301 was the statute under U.S. law dealing with "unfair" foreign trade practices and measures to be taken to combat them. Major changes were made to Section 301 under the Trade Act of 1988. The Trade Act also introduced a new procedure, the so-called "Super 301," whereby the U.S. Trade Representative was required to identify priority unfair trade practices and priority foreign countries and initiate Section 301 investigations with a view to negotiating an agreement to eliminate or compensate for the alleged foreign practice. If no agreement was reached with the foreign country concerned, then unilateral retaliatory action had to be taken.

An additional new provision was the "Special-301" procedure concerning intellectual property (IP) protection. This provision required the administration to identify priority foreign nations it considered to be denying adequate IP rights to U.S. firms. This could under certain conditions have led to unilateral measures by the United States.

Unilateral action under Section 301 on the basis of a unilateral determination without authorization from the GATT contracting parties had been declared illegal by most nations in their interpretation of GATT. Such unilateral action, they believe, ran counter to basic GATT principles and they believed was in clear violation of specific provisions of the General Agreement. Except in the fields of dumping and subsidization, where autonomous action is possible, measures taken against other parties must be sanctioned by the GATT Contracting Parties.

The U.S. used the Section 301 procedure twice against the European Community in 1989: first on January 1, when retaliatory measures were introduced against the E.C. in the well-publicized hormones dispute, and then, on July 5, when the United States Trade Representative made a determination of unfairness with respect to the E.C. oilseeds regime. Additionally, the United States had repeatedly used the threat of Section 301 action in 1989, in flagrant violation of GATT rules. The disputes concerning canned fruit, shipbuilding, and Airbus were cases in point. According to the European Community and other foreign governments Section 301 has been used to the detriment of their trading rights, which they will aggressively defend.

In 1990 the Super 301 provision of the 1988 trade legislation expired.

Some Congressional leaders were convinced that it was the most successful provision of the 1988 trade act and want it back, with better enforcement provisions. United States trade representative Carla A. Hills said there was "already an ample arsenal of tools," and expressed the opinion that Super 301 was actually "quite clumsy" because it required initiation of the process on a specific date.

Should GATT survive, many U.S. lawmakers are convinced that Super 301 (or something similar to it) should be re-enacted as the price Congress exacts for approving any global agreement. Historically, when Congress gets a trade policy shift, there is usually some improved protection for domestic industry and workers, in return for supporting international agreements that open the U.S. to more imports. Assuredly world trade will not collapse, but trade wars will surely intensify, and a promising ladder out of poverty will have been ripped from under the world's poorest nations.

Protectionism is certainly alive and well. Now it is the United States' turn. Given that the European Community was launched and supported with U.S. financial and morale incentives; given that Japan is our closest ally in the Pacific, there is a remarkable amount of suspicion, contempt, and even downright hatred in the air.

The chairman of Sony, Akio Morita, and a politician, Shintaro Ishihara, wrote the book *The Japan that Can Say No* in 1989. Many in Japan believe it is about time that it stand up for itself when dealing with the U.S. For the book's authorized English translation, Mr. Morita hastily withdrew the chapters of the book he authored for fear of the damage it might do to Sony's sales. In turn, Mr. Ishihara added five new chapters to the English edition, consisting mostly of advice to America to balance his previous advice to Japan. Putting the significantly distorted facts of the book aside, it is illustrative of a rapidly changing wind spreading throughout Japan.

One reason the U.S. Congress, especially the Democrats, want to revise Super 301 is the resentment toward Japan's halfhearted support for Operation Desert Storm in 1991. During the 10 days of wide-ranging trade talks, Japanese officials told U.S. negotiators, in effect, that Tokyo was doing the U.S. a huge favor by sticking with the gulf coalition and pledging $13 billion toward the war effort. The Japanese made it clear they would rather pay higher oil prices than see supplies jeopardized by a long war. Tokyo thought it had done its part and saw little need to offer new trade concessions. Two years of talks on U.S. access to the Japanese construction market had produced little but acrimony. Despite promises, U.S. firms had won less than $200 million worth of work, while Japanese contractors do $2.5 billion a year of business in the U.S.

In addition, claims of Fortress Europe, Europe for Europeans, quotas, protectionism, subsidies, etc. being echoed in the hallowed European

Community headquarters in Brussels add fuel to the fire. A response of significance is called for. The "sleeping giant" slumbers no more. A forward thinking free-trade policy of economic union is called for with our North American, and later Latin American neighbors to protect the future. We have long shared our wealth with others. We have at the same time benefited from such philanthrophy. Nevertheless, the time may be fast approaching when we must seek ways to insulate ourselves against a determined maneuver by our equally clever counterparts around the world who are more interested in their own piety and rules of play as memories of our past help to once humbled nations fade quickly.

6

TOWARD ECONOMIC UNION—ESTABLISHING FREE-TRADE ACCORDS

CANADA AND A FREE-TRADE ACCORD

In early November 1988 Canadian voting citizens were in the midst of the most rancorous general election in their 121-year history. Polls showed that they remained deeply divided over a proposed trade accord with the United States. Opinion surveys conducted in the last hours of the campaign gave the party that negotiated the trade pact, the governing Progressive Conservatives, a lead of 5 to 11 percentage points over its main opponents, the Liberals.

Prime Minister Brian Mulroney, the leader of the Conservatives, was bolstered by the polls. "Scare tactics," as he described them, including allegations that it would wreck social programs and throw Canadians out of work, had failed. With all the bitterness, Canada's 17 million registered voters were left with little doubt that they faced an eventual choice. By electing a Parliament that could approve the trade agreement, the public would commit the country over 10 years to what President Reagan had called "a new economic order for North America."

Advocates of the trade deal saw a continental marketplace of 267 million people in which Canadian and American entrepreneurs would be equal competitors. A loss in the election would send the message that Canadians would opt for a continuation of Canada's protectionist policies. It was a watershed that Canadians had reached at least three times, in 1891, 1911, and 1947. Each time they rejected closer economic ties with their more powerful and populous southern neighbor, the United States.

Opponents of the deal raised doubts that Canada's expensive social programs, like universal medical care, could survive open competition with the United States. Critics said that Mr. Mulroney surrendered too much in guaranteeing the U.S. access to Canada's energy resources at prices no higher than those paid by Canadians. The opposition to the pact was bitter even though more than 80 percent of United States-Canadian trade was already duty free.

Canada was by 1988 in its sixth year of an economic boom that had lowered unemployment to less than 8 percent, considered relatively low in Canada. The boom was expected to produce a real annual growth rate that year of 4 percent, one of the highest rates in the western world. Inflation was at 4 percent, but the growth was uneven. However, the annual deficit was at $24 billion, almost 50 percent higher, proportional to Canada's population of 26 million, than the U.S. deficit.

The idea for the trade pact was a Canadian initiative. In 1985 there was great concern that Congress, trying to cope with America's progressively larger trade deficits, would write protectionist legislation that would cut Canada out of its bigger foreign market, where eighty percent of Canada's exports go to the United States.

President Reagan and Prime Minister Mulroney agreed in March of 1985 that the two nations would "explore all possible ways" of reducing trade barriers. On October 4, 1987, the two governments concluded a free-trade agreement. The accord would end all tariffs on the trade between the nations, estimated at $150 billion per year, over a ten-year period beginning in January 1989. The agreement also lowered or eliminated trade barriers on energy and agriculture, eased restrictions on U.S. investment in Canada, and allowed for easier flows into service industries, including banking and finance. The agreement was passed by both houses of Congress and signed by President Reagan in September 1988. On November 21st, the people ended the bitter campaign with a stunning victory for Mulroney, thus insuring ratification of the free-trade agreement—a free market across the 49th Parallel.

The free-trade agreement would take effect on January 1, 1989 with expectations that it would also lead to significant changes in the world trading system. With the accord, both the United States and Canada had formalized what is already the largest trading relationship between the two nations. The agreement was expected to reduce both countries' cost of doing business, increasing their productivity and competitiveness. The agreement would reduce inflation, create more jobs, and strengthen Canada's economy. But it would also increase the government deficit by over $4.2 billion by 1997, which would lead to higher taxes.

At the same time, Canada would get increased access to a market 10 times its size. In return it would make the bigger tariff cuts because its tariffs were three to four times higher than those of the United States. Most economists concluded that in 10 years, with the agreement in full force, Canada's economy would expand 5 percent faster than it would have otherwise, with the American economy growing 1 percent faster. One result would be the hundreds of thousands of additional jobs created on both sides of the border. The Agreement with Ottawa would have a major effect on multinational corporate strategy. A company that has production and distribution in both the United States and Canada previously had to pay duties when its goods crossed the border. Such duties hindered what otherwise would have been unencumbered access to labor, raw materials, and other economic resources. Now, these barriers had been wiped away.

By January 1, 1991 when Canada's Goods and Services Tax, a 7 percent value-added tax, went into effect, it began to alter the terms of the free-trade accord in Canada's favor, creating claims by some in the United States for a U.S. value-added tax system. This broad-based sales tax allowed Canadian exporters to get a rebate equal to the amount of the tax they have paid on purchases related to their foreign sales, so they are able to sell their goods abroad for less than previously. Because the new tax substitutes for a manufacturers excise tax that was not refundable and had reached as high as 13.5 percent, Canadian manufacturers could become more competitive. This new tax increased Canadian exports by more than $1.25 billion in American dollars annually for several years. All in all, this will increase Canada's trade surplus with the United States and raise disturbing counter-demands from U.S. citizens and politicians.

The free-trade agreement was widely expected to trigger cross-border shakeouts. But as the unified market unfolded between the two nations, a wave of consolidations occurred faster and earlier than anyone had predicted. Canada's tariffs against U.S. washing machines, for example, were scheduled to be phased out over 10 years, but Whirlpool decided to act years earlier. The free-trade accord eliminated, for example, Canada's 8 percent duty on American-made motorcycles. Under the agreement, all remaining tariffs would be abolished over 10 years. In the first round the pact eliminated a 3.9 percent tariff on U.S. computers shipped to Canada as well as 4.9 percent to 22 percent duties on trade in whiskey, skates, furs, and unprocessed fish. The result will be that retail prices on these products should drop in both countries.

In industry after industry, Canadian firms are merging among themselves or with U.S. firms to form giants. The push appears to be accelerating with requests to speed up the phaseout of tariffs on company products. Canadian executives rushed across the border to set up manufacturing bases in what they saw as a more hospitable climate. Analysts expected a double-digit percentage gain in Canadian investment in America in 1989, to more than $41 billion. The surprising shift to U.S. production by potentially large numbers of firms comes as Canada's exports to its nearest neighbor were flattening out.

By 1989, Mulroney had failed to convince many Canadians that free-trade was a good thing. The Canadian Labor Congress had claimed that tariffs that were dropped in that year had already cost 50,000 jobs. While American exports to Canada had risen, the rate of increase of Canadian exports had slowed. In the first quarter, Canada's surplus with the U.S. had sagged to $2.8 billion reflecting a 27 percent reduction over the same period two years earlier. Many Canadians have come to believe that freer competition will lead to a harsh society.

By mid-year 1991, hundreds of national companies began to abandon Canada to move south of the border to the U.S. They were attracted by lower American wages, more modest personal and business taxes, and cheaper real estate. Canadian labor officials claimed that about 200,000 positions had already been lost by this shift of operations.

To fight back, the Canadian government replaced its old manufacturers tax with a lower goods-and-services tax that is refunded when goods are exported. (Although the particulars differ, Mexico is watching this trend and is anxious that its free-trade accord with the U.S. and Canada could also create an exodus of industry northward.)

Caring or not, the reshuffling of the U.S.-Canadian economy will continue. The two nations already are the world's largest trading partners, doing at least $150 billion worth of business a year with each other. The results of the free-trade pact are so encouraging that both nations have agreed to accelerate tariff cutting under the new agreement. Prime Minister Mulroney seeks to eliminate 500 provincial trade barriers by the middle of the decade. Were he to be successful and correct, Canada will reap a reward of billions of dollars of added output and thousands of new jobs.

Part of the agenda, though hardly stated in public, is to help both nations meet intensified competition from Asia and the European Community. Attention would next turn south of the border, where another accord would fit into the puzzle of free-trade and prosperity.

MEXICO AND A FREE-TRADE ACCORD

While the GATT meetings were collapsing in Brussels at the end of 1990, President Bush was laying the groundwork for an alternative U.S. trade strategy. His six-day tour of South America (delayed because of the Middle-East crisis in Kuwait) promoted his *Enterprise for the Americas*, a set of sweeping proposals to lower trade and investment barriers between the U.S. and Latin American nations.

By 1990 Mexico, with its population of 86 million and GNP of $201 billion, shared in the economy of North America with a trade to the U.S. equal to $52 billion and to Canada at $2.3 billion. Trade between the U.S.

and Mexico reached more than $50 billion, up from $29.7 billion in 1986. In 1990, of the $393 billion U.S. exports, 7.2 percent went to Mexico, while of Mexico's $22 billion total exports, 71 percent went to the United States, that is, the U.S. gets 71 cents of each dollar that Mexicans spend on imports.

Thousands of American manufacturers, from small producers to major players in corporate America are now pouring into Mexico for low-cost labor. For the first time in a century, south of the border was starting to look like one of the world's best places for Americans to conduct business. Open markets, cheap labor, and a government that appears to be delivering both economic and political security are the key to the three-nation game strategy.

Since the late 1980s Mexico's dramatic reform suggests a dissolution of the 2,000 mile border with the U.S. At first, it only appeared to be a maneuver to upgrade Mexican living standards. This was the case. But then in the summer of 1990, Presidents Bush and Salinas announced a program to forge ahead with a free-trade pact. For Carlos Salinas, his goal of a free-trading Mexico is to divert funds and technology from the United States that is presently leaving for low-cost havens in Asia and Central Europe.

In November 1990 Mexico extended through the end of 1991 its Pact for Stability and Economic Growth, a program that has reduced inflation to less than 30 percent in 1990 from triple digits in 1987. In the fifth extension of the agreement with labor and business leaders, the government reduced to 40 centavos a day the current 80-centavos-a-day programmed rate at which the peso is devalued against the U.S. dollar. The peso is now valued at about 3,000 to the dollar. The minimum wage was raised by 18 percent, less than expected. There were increases in prices; those increases were to be offset by tax breaks and by expanding distribution of subsidized milk and tortillas to low-income districts.

The six trillion dollar gamble of North America will be a strong and compelling match for Asia and Europe. Mexico is central to its success. No oceans need be crossed, nor planes required to traverse borders, but good roads and highways will link the nations.

With her literacy rate of 87 percent of the working population, Mexico is well-positioned to yield high productivity with the lowest wages found in any industrialized western nation. For example, compared with other low-cost nations, the average hours wage plus benefits in 1989 were: Mexico $1.63, Singapore $2.25, South Korea $2.94, and Taiwan $3.71. And when compared to the U.S.'s $14.32 the figures are impressive as a magnet to attract the building and expansion of U.S. subsidiaries and joint-ventures with Mexican industrialists. In the past four years, U.S. trade with Mexico has tripled, to $60 billion, with Mexico importing nearly as much as Japan.

On still another front is the historic breakthrough in Mexico's economic transition. Never before has a developing nation with a booming population and an extremely low wage scale entered into free trade with a major industrial player. Since the 1970s U.S. firms, along with some Japanese and European companies, have opened more than 1,900 assembly plants close to the U.S. border. The maquiladoras which are growing at a 15 percent annual clip, employ half a million Mexicans, paying them an average of $5 a day, with free lunch. (The Mexican government makes the maquiladora an exception to nationalistic restrictions on 100 percent foreign ownership and also offers duty-free importation of high-quality components and machinery.) The United States and other foreign firms send $12 billion in parts to these so-called screwdriver assembly plants which are mostly foreign operations on Mexican soil, where plants purchase 97 percent of their parts from the U.S. and sell almost none of their efforts within Mexico. United States Tariff Items 9802.00.60 and 9802.00.80 allow for duty-free entry into the U.S. of goods assembled in another country from components of U.S. origin. Duty is only paid on components that are not of U.S. origin, and the value added in assembly or manufacture in Mexico.

By the end of 1990 there were nearly 2,000 maquiladora plants operating in Mexico, with 468,773 workers. The industry each year now generates more than $12.4 billion in products and over $3 billion of value-added income for Mexico. It ranks second only to petroleum as a generator of foreign exchange.

A proposed free-trade accord will rapidly alter this activity, changing such plants to regional firms that buy and sell on both sides of the border. Within a decade, continued changes would lead to free-trade promoters, making assembly parts in regional areas that are among Mexico's poorest and trucking these items closer to the U.S. border for assembly.

According to a March 1991 poll taken by the new Mexican journal *Este País*, close to 80 percent of Mexicans favor a trade agreement with the United States and Canada, what one phrase-maker calls a zone from the Yukon to the Yucatan. There is the belief that open competition, not traditionally encouraged in Mexico, will become firmly entrenched within the domestic economy.

Unfortunately, the agreement's primary impact will be on the "tradable" portion of the economy, while most economic assets in Mexico, and other developing nations, are in "non-tradable" goods. Pricing on these items is outside the sphere of external competition. For example, agricultural products are considered tradable, but what makes them possible, the market for arable land, is not.

Nevertheless, the Salinas gamble appears to be succeeding, well beyond the screwdriver mentality of the past decade. For example, 950 miles south of El Paso, Guadalajara is evolving as Mexico's Silicon Valley, with major American computer firms, such as IBM, Hewlett-Packard, and

Wang, producing computers there for domestic and export consumption. Ford Motor Company, attracted in part by only having to pay $2.50 an hour in wages, uses Mexicans to assemble cars and components. Today, Ford, having spent almost $1 billion on its export facility in Hermosillo, produces Mercury Tracers for the U.S.

Agriculturally, Mexico is fast becoming the U.S.'s salad bowl. Since 1985, U.S. imports of Mexican food have more than doubled, to $2.6 billion. Mexico now provides 25 percent of the $5.4 billion worth of fruit and vegetables imported annually to the United States. And this will certainly grow more rapidly as the free-trade accord evolves. With wages on farms set between $4 and $5 a day vs. the typical minimum U.S. wage of $3.65 per hour, even major U.S. food companies have begun to process items south of the border and then ship them north. For example, Pillsbury Company moved most of its Green Giant frozen broccoli and cauliflower production from California to Mexico, with a loss of 375 jobs. Eight hundred Mexicans were hired in Irapuato, Guanajuato, 150 miles north of Mexico City.

In order to survive, some 18 of the 40 board members of the Western Growers Association now farm in Mexico. The free-trade accord will eliminate approximately 15 percent of the food tariffs between the two nations. This gain for Mexico terrifies U.S. growers. Florida and California orange growers will probably lose their 35 percent tariff on Mexican equivalent fruits. The tradeoff, also lost under the free-trade agreement, will be the surrendering of the tariffs for importing nearly half of Mexican imported staples of U.S. corn, wheat, and beans. In addition, Mexico is one of the world's largest importers of milk, mostly from U.S. dairies. The inevitable is upon us. Gradual unification of North American agriculture will arrive shortly.

While most fruit and vegetable growers in northern Mexico like the idea of exporting to the U.S. without the quotas and the tariffs of up to 37.6 percent that would follow a free-trade accord, other farmers throughout the country worry. For example, about 2.6 million Mexicans farm maize. Part of the Mexican national identity grew out of their domestication of the plant.

President Salinas opened farming to international competition by lowering tariffs and abolishing import licenses for all except four basic products, wheat, maize, beans, and powdered milk, although plans to lift the license on wheat have been cancelled. Unsubsidized farmers would be devastated. He has cut tariffs and phased out subsidies on farm inputs such as fertilizers. Guaranteed prices have been eliminated, except for maize and beans. The government has privatized state food-processing firms. The success of these policies has been to lower inflation and the government deficit.

Since the 1910–20 revolution, which was partially a peasant uprising against the seizure of ancestral lands by the larger landowners, the nation's constitution limited the size of private farms. More than half of the land, some of it expropriated, was given to landless peasants organized in farming communities called *ejidos*. This land belongs to the nation. *Ejido* farmers are allowed to use it and bequeath the right to use it, but not to sell, mortgage, or rent it. (Foreign ownership or investment in the *ejidos* is also prohibited, a concern to many in the United States.) These farmers, nearly 2 million who grow maize, are a political force of the ruling Institutional Revolutionary Party (PRI).

During the 1980s, public investment in farming dropped by four-fifths, with rural credit dropping by more than a half. With government spending sharply down, farmers suffered, the population increased significantly, and Mexico became a net importer of food. The president of Mexico is well aware that reforming small farming may be a formidable challenge.

By 1991 President Salinas's plan to transform Mexican agriculture had quickly become a potential brake in his quest to modernize the economy. His agrarian reform was touching the very heart of Mexican history of the last 70 years. In early November, 2.5 million peasants still waiting for their plots of redistributed wealth in the countryside were told that there was no more land to give away.

All is tense. While farmers and their families make up nearly a third of the nation's people, they produce less than one-tenth of the gross national product and have collected less than 1 percent of the billions of dollars in foreign investment flowing into Mexico.

In addition, the president moved to legalize the sale of redistributed land and to permit large-scale agribusiness ventures, with foreigners free to participate. Within a decade or two, it is projected that half of Mexico's poverty stricken farmers will most likely be forced to leave their land.

Of course, the U.S. government, prodded by unions and many industrialists who fear American job losses, will seek tough rules of origin to guarantee that Mexican output won't saturate the U.S. market. U.S. unions argue that the Mexican free-trade accord will depress U.S. wages and send jobs fleeing south of the border where firms will benefit from repression, corruption, and lax work standards.

Such fears are misconceived. Trade does indeed tend to uproot production from one region to another; that is, in part, its purpose. However, work that can be done more cheaply in Mexico than in the U.S. should be. Shifting some of America's production to Mexico will not make us poorer; but quite the opposite. The labor and capital it once employed unproductively would move to new and better uses, and demand higher wages.

Trade alters the work that people do, usually for the better. It does not make them unemployable. As our southern neighbor prospers, its people will insist on healthier and safer jobs. There is no surer way to make Mexico a perplexing and disturbed neighbor that to keep it destitute.

Nevertheless, to get fast-track approval from Congress in May 1991, the Bush Administration announced that it would pay for some retraining of U.S. workers displaced by the free-trade accord with Mexico. On the first of the month, the president offered concessions to pick up support for the Mexican-U.S. trade accord by pledging:

1. to work with Congress to fashion an "adequately funded" program of assistance for workers dislocated as a result of increased foreign competition.
2. to exclude changes in immigration policy from the trade pact.
3. to prevent Mexican products that do not meet U.S. health or safety requirements from entering this country.
4. to put in place an integrated environmental plan for the border between the U.S. and Mexico and appoint representatives of environmental organizations to official trade advisory bodies.

President Bush's action plan played a critical vote on extending his trade-negotiating authority for two more years.

Negotiations pushed man's mettle to a fine line when it came to formulating how products enjoying Mexico's easy access would have to be made primarily from U.S. parts. Those with high Asian or European content would face U.S. import duties. In addition, U.S. trade negotiators demanded a pact to provide legal protection for our patents and technology within Mexico. And they will certainly want to get Salinas to eliminate the remaining constitutional restrictions on foreign investment within his borders.

Of special interest to the United States, but also to other nations, especially Japan, are her vast crude oil reserves. Mexico has the fourth largest oil reserves in the world. Should Mexico make its crude oil more available to Japan on the open market, Japan would be forever thankful for being able to reduce, if not nearly eliminate, its dependence on Middle East production.

What remains as a controversial point in any free-trade agreement are the stinking border towns in Mexico laced with toxic industrial pollutants and untreated sewage. This runaway pollution and accompanying health threats are found in virtually every community along the Mexican border with the U.S. For example, a health emergency has been in force on the Arizona side of Mexico for six months in 1991 because the incidence of hepatitis had climbed to 20 times the national average. The major non-economic fear is that the accord will ignite a rush to develop more industries and spawn new wastes.

Environmental border catastrophes are raising cries from environmentalists. Across the Rio Grande from El Paso, Texas, rubber tires are burned in kilns that make decorative tiles and bricks. And furniture-making plants and metal-plating shops that have fled environmental restrictions in California, now flourish in Tijuana, Mexico, producing toxic wastes from their use of solvents. All this continues to frustrate free-trade supporters.

The administrator of the U.S. Environmental Protection Agency, William Reilly, argues " . . . I believe the economic opportunities arising from a free-trade agreement would offer an unprecedented chance to improve environmental protection, not just along the border, but throughout Mexico." And for those American firms rushing to Mexico to escape pollution regulations in the United States, the chief air-pollution monitor for Mexico City declared that any company seeking to relocate to Mexico would have to comply with emission standards at least as strict as where it came from, and possibly more so.

Both the U.S. and Mexico released a draft plan on August 1, 1991 to improve the quality of the environment along their common borders. The document called for extra investment in wastewater treatment plants, greater restrictions on hazardous-waste shipments across the border, and the hiring of more officials to enforce environmental laws in Mexico. William Reilly then sent letters to about 150 U.S. firms that operate manufacturing assembly plants in northern Mexico asking for voluntary efforts to reduce their emissions of 17 toxic chemicals from these plants by a third before the end of 1992 and by 50 percent before the end of 1995.

"Parallelism" is a concept that demands a tradeoff. A free-trade agreement gets signed, with the mutually involved countries commiting themselves to cooperation on improving the environment. In the long-run, such an approach could become the model throughout the hemisphere.

The struggle for environmental protection will be fought across Central and South America. As Mexico goes, so might the rest of the Latin American nations in the future. Environmentalists push their argument forward insisting that Mexico's less stringent pollution and environmental laws would attract American and Canadian industries seeking to avoid controls at home.

The U.S.-Canadian free-trade agreement made the crossover to Mexico nearly inevitable. What is clear is that the free-trade pact with our southern neighbor will spark a new wave of U.S. investment in Mexico, where labor costs are significantly different, as compared with similarities between the U.S. and Canada. The accord with Mexico will create the flow of dollars with its apparent tradeoffs, at least in the short run, of American higher unemployment. Competitive and labor-intensive industries, such as automobile and appliance manufacturing, will mushroom along and beyond the border. By concentrating the production of such items in one area, firms will generate economies of scale giving them hopefully a world-class competitive edge. With time, as wages upgrade throughout Mexico and get closer to those of northern nations, the attraction will slow down, leaving Mexicans with new industries and a raised standard of living.

As barriers are lifted, trade and investment will expand, stimulating growth in the United States. Mexican demand for machinery and transportation equipment will escalate. The free-trade pact should boost R&D at firms headquartered throughout the U.S. but operating plants in Mexico. U.S. service industries, such as banking, insurance, telecommunications, etc., will receive a comparable expansion.

One further obstacle to a successful free-trade accord is Mexico's obsolete legal system. In the U.S., between 1985 and 1989, there were more than 6,000 cases where one business charged another with monopoly or unfair business practices. In the same time period in Mexico, there were none. The monopoly laws of Mexico do not presently ensure equal opportunity, where market distortions and monopoly business practices are the rule and not the exception.

As Alejandro Junco, publisher of *El Norte* newspaper wrote in March 1991, "establishing competitive internal markets in a traditionally noncompetitive society is a far more complicated matter than just signing free-trade agreements and privatizing state industries. In the long term, it is not enough that our products be allowed to compete freely; it is the societies that make those products that must be allowed to do so." These Napoleonic laws need to be altered.

Probably the greatest challenge for the two presidents and their bureaucrats was to find a way to open up Mexico's undercapitalized oil industry to American investment—which is presently prohibited by Mexican law. The tradeoff may come in a softening by the U.S. and a gradual tearing down of U.S. quotas on textiles and steel along with opening U.S. markets to currently prohibited Mexican fruits and vegetables. Mexico grows more avocados than any nation in the world but presently sells none in the United States.

The transition will be bumpy for Mexico as well as for the United States, strategically sandwiched between Canada and Mexico. A decade of balancing acts will descend on the capitals of the U.S. and Mexico. Americans will fear job losses to Mexico and Mexicans are already phobic about becoming a satellite or even possibly the 51st annexation.

In November 1990, President Bush with President Salinas was promised approval of a law protecting intellectual property rights in Mexico, a major victory for U.S. firms wishing to invest there. In addition, they both discussed a precedent-setting, multibillion-dollar line of financing from the U.S. Export-Import Bank that would pave the way for American oil-service companies to help Mexico's nationalized oil companies develop Mexican oil fields.

Once the free-trade accord with Mexico is implemented the passage of time will show its positive contributions. "Made in North America," will be the commonplace label on the way to forging the greater New American Community.

And what of Canada in all of this? It too will benefit from Mexico's rising prosperity rather than suffer from it. Presently, Canada's trade with Mexico amounts to a fraction of its business with the U.S. Canadian exports to Mexico in 1990 totaled only $517.8 million, less than 0.5 percent of Canada's total exports of $123.04 billion. Canada's imports from Mexico in 1990 totalled $1.5 billion, or 1.3 percent of Canada's total imports of $118,473 billion.

Canadian firms will exploit opportunities presented to them by a neighboring nation that at long last not only has some money to spend, but that has discarded its erstwhile protectionist shell. Building Mexico's infrastructure remains the principal source of business opportunities for Canadian companies for the coming decade. Whether through joint ventures or by establishing operations in Mexico, both Canadian and U.S. firms are scrambling to get a chunk of the $20 billion earmarked to be spent on its infrastructure. Canadian officials see Mexico as a potentially large purchaser of Canadian goods, such as newsprint, mining products, mass transit, and telecommunications equipment.

And certainly, Canada as a result of participating in the U.S.-Mexican negotiations, by necessity must alter some of its earlier agreements with the United States. Thus the older trade accord with Canada would require some "enhancements," thus balancing out forces to create a more equitable trade agreement.

A war in the Persian Gulf did not halt President Bush from telling reporters on February 5, 1991 of his plans to have all three interested parties participate together in creating a combined market of 360 million consumers with an annual output of nearly $6 trillion.

More than ever, the Mexican economy showed signs of preparing for a trade accord with the U.S. Its stock market index had approximately doubled since July 1989, outperforming every other market in the world. On January 19, 1990, with considerable fanfare, the Salinas government published its "National Program for Modernization of Industry and Foreign Trade." It served to prepare the Mexican people for a free-trade accord with the U.S.

One week later the Minister of Trade and Industry proposed major revisions in laws protecting intellectual property be introduced to the Mexican Congress. Its slowness in being introduced and the debate that it fostered only illustrated the complexities and difficulties of Mexican reform in general. Once it was recognized by Mexican politicians that protecting U.S. intellectual property would increase the flow to Mexico of technology greatly needed for economic development, new provisions were introduced.

On May 14, 1990, Mexico's Congress voted a constitutional amendment to privatize banking, thus marking a historical moment in its history as profound as any. Yes, problems remain including a 14 percent annual crawling-peg devaluation of the peso. Nevertheless the most impressive aspect of Mexico's ascent during the late 1980s and early 1990s was the way in which the supposedly insuperable problems of foreign debt and government deficits melted away, virtually unnoticed. Inflation was brought to below 20 percent from over 150 percent, the peso became stable, foreign-exchange reserves increased, and the short-term Treasury bill rate was down to 34 percent—despite the fact that Mexico has received virtually no new loans from commercial banks.

In 1991, the Mexican government took dramatic steps to set things right, with a swiftness and resolve for other Latin American nations. Mexico has already taken the following steps:

1. reduced the top marginal tax rate to 35 percent, the latest in a series of gradual reductions, from 60 percent in 1986;
2. abolished the special tax status of small companies, a first step toward integrating them into the mainstream economy, so they can grow and combine into larger enterprises;
3. abolished similar special tax status for transportation and agricultural firms;
4. threw out a huge number of offensive regulations, notably most restrictions on foreign investment, transportation regulations, protection of the state petrochemical monopoly, and so forth;
5. eliminated most of the remaining nontariff barriers to trade, including domestic-content quotas for cars and electronics;
6. sold off the majority of state industrial holdings—the big exception is and remains Pemex, the national oil firm.

Mexico has been on a fast track for ten years. The sale of its telephone company brought in about $6 billion. Its 18 state-run banks are being sold, with three of them, Banco Mercantil, Banco Cremi, and Banpais, put on the block in 1991. Sidermex, Mexico's steel company should fetch $2 billion. Since it started privatization in 1983 more than 170 of Mexico's companies have been sold for more than $8 billion. And lest we in America fail to capitalize on her internationalizing of trade, Mexico in April 1991 signed a cooperation accord with the European Community that it hopes will increase its trade with the 12-nation bloc.

On the negative side, Mexico must still grapple with the approximately 14 percent per annum rate of devaluation of the peso, the barring of foreigners from majority ownership of mining firms, oil exploration, development, refining, and retailing monopolies. Income taxes are still too high even though the top marginal rate has dropped to 35 percent, it applies to annual income in excess of $7,000 (in the U.S. a family earning $7,000 would pay no taxes at all), thus continuing to encourage small businesses from remaining off the books and hiring workers without reporting their incomes.

One big question hanging over investment in Mexico is whether inflation can be held in check. An accord of the late 1980s among government, business, and labor, brought inflation down from 160 percent to today's 17 percent annual rate. For if Mexico's economy doesn't move into manageable growth without inflation, Mexico's investment pitch may lose its allure to the world.

In the 1990s, Mexico may easily duplicate or even better the experience of the Asian tigers during the 1980s. Mexico's growth rate should be at least 7 percent, the growth rate between 1960 and 1980, and it could exceed 10 percent. It could easily have the fastest-growing economy in the hemisphere.

Clearly, the economic outlook for Mexico appears sound. During the first six months of 1991 the local stock market was up 73 percent in dollar terms. The nation's current account deficit has risen steadily, to a projected $7 billion in 1991 from $1.7 billion in 1986. Inflation has been falling, down to 29.9 percent in 1990 from 160 percent in 1987. By the end of 1991 the inflation rate slipped below 20 percent.

In May of 1991, Congress gave President Bush fast- track authority to negotiate with Mexico for a free-trade agreement, subject to congressional approval without amendments. The House of Representatives on May 23rd backed the president's authority 231 to 192, while the Senate vote on May 24th was 59 to 36. In return, President Bush made two pledges, one to include environmental representation on his advisory committee on trade policy and negotiation and the other to consult closely with Congress throughout the negotiations for a free-trade agreement with Mexico.

The Mexican government is banking on free-trade as its last step to recovery. As President Salinas said, "Mexico wants trade not aid." Everything else is in place. Workers have benefited from the growth Mexico had recorded in 1990 and 1991. The program that cut inflation to less than 20 percent in 1990 from 170 percent in 1987 has helped bring a critical recuperation in purchasing power. Workers in Mexico can now earn as much as they did before the debt crisis, and most manufacturers now pay double the minimum wage to attract help. Under a U.S. free-trade accord Mexico will raise its growth rate by an extra 1.2 percent to more than 5 percent through the first five years of the pact. With an economy twenty-five times smaller than that of the United States, the projected accord should pose no major threat from Mexico's signing.

The goal will be met as an outgrowth of a comprehensive North American trade agreement linking 360 million people of the United States, Canada, and Mexico, who produce nearly $6 trillion of goods and services each year.

By October 1991 trade negotiations in Zacatecas, Mexico were moving ahead. Issues of rules of origin were debated including determining how much North American content a product would have to have to qualify for tariff breaks under any agreement. Differences between U.S.-Canadian and Mexican legal systems dovetail into the handling of unfair-trade complaints remained to be clarified along with tensions over agriculture, textiles, and steel practices.

At the same time, President Salinas continued to outline further programs for change throughout Mexico. Following the support generated from recent regional elections he proudly announced that the nation's economic growth for the first half of 1991 had approached an impressive 5 percent on an annual basis. The 11.9 percent inflation in the first nine months of the year was the country's lowest in 16 years. And to encourage popular support in his nation and around the world, the president took credit for the foreign exchange reserves rising to the highest in Mexico's history, nearly doubling in one year to $16.1 billion from $8.415 billion the year before. One of Salinas's last imaginative actions of 1991 was to fire nearly all of the country's customs inspectors and replace them to combat corruption and improve efficiency. The new nonunion customs force would receive higher salaries and be rotated often to foil criminal ties with importers.

Throughout the bumpy ride to implementation and evaluation, there now is this model staring at the rest of the Americas. The economic future of Central and South American nations will increasingly depend on participation in the path prepared for them by the North American Community. A North American Free Trade Area awaits the hemispheres. Hopefully, countries south of Mexico will study all the negotiated free-trade accords very carefully. Their turn must soon come. The stakes are high, as other nations will have to watch that their outdated nationalistic notions do not stand in the way of a united free-trade front, serving both individual and collective interests of countries.

THE AMERICAS AS ONE

The U.S. has long maintained a trade relationship with Latin America and in this century supplanted Europe in economic importance. By 1914, the United States were purchasing 75 percent of Mexico's exports and supplying 50 percent of its neighbor's imports. By 1919 the United States consumed two-thirds of Central America's exports, while furnishing that area with three-quarters of its imports.

Forty years later, realizing that the majority of Latin Americans wanted change, President John F. Kennedy, fearful that Cuba's Fidel Castro's form of communism might be the preferred choice, devised an imaginative plan in 1961 for a democratic evolution. He launched his Alliance for Progress, a program to encourage economic development, to promote the growth of democracy, and to urge social justice. It failed for being too theoretical and unstructured on one level, too revolutionary on another.

The long-standing oligarchy had no intention of freely volunteering to give away or sell its land holdings, to tax itself more heavily, or to share its power with a broader population. On March 13, 1971, the tenth anniversary of the Alliance for Progress passed unnoticed.

Throughout the decade of the sixties, there were more military dictatorships and less evidence of democracy. Military dominance replaced thirteen constitutional governments, and the United States found itself lavishly supporting these military dictators, where two-thirds of Alliance for Progress monies went to these military-controlled governments. In 1979 only Colombia, Venezuela, Guyana, Suriname, and French Guiana were civilian-controlled governments in all of South America. (By 1991, only Suriname was a military-run government.) After nearly $10 billion of investment in Latin America, economically, growth per capita during the decade averaged only 1.8 percent, lower than it was in the years before the alliance was signed.

Another twenty years were to pass before a new, formal economic policy based on the lowering of trade barriers was attempted. In June 1990, President Bush said of his scheme that "the future of Latin America lies with free government and free markets" and that "we must forge a genuine partnership for free market reform." He proposed a "free trade zone from the port of Anchorage to the Tierra del Fuego." And as many economists argue, Latin America holds the key to the U.S. trade deficit.

Latin American leaders are leaving their traditional statism protectionism for capitalism. South American nations are cutting tariffs and subsidies, selling off state-run businesses, and turning to private investment as the stimulus for economic expansion, forming a picture that the northern and southern hemisphere's economies are overlapping and increasingly similar. The result is likely to be a considerable expansion of the already $120 billion in two-way trade between the U.S. and Latin American nations.

Part of Bush's strategy is a $1.5 billion fund, with some contributions coming from both Japan and Europe. It would ensure that economic reforms would continue by improving conditions for private investment— for example, by helping pay for the retraining of workers laid off by privatizations, already a significant new feature of change. There are also efforts to ease the region's staggering debt burden, particularly in smaller nations. The U.S. has offered concessions on repayment of the $12 billion owed to U.S. government agencies.

By far the biggest thrust to new trade and investment is a series of bilateral "framework agreements" that the U.S. has signed with individual nations. They purport to provide a mechanism for lowering trade and investment barriers on a case-by-case basis. For example, a new accord with Chile—one of six signed so far—spells out an "immediate action agenda." The U.S. will look for ways to ease nontariff barriers against

Chilean farm products in return for better protection of intellectual property rights of foreign firms in Chile.

This agreement in turn, stirred a move by Chile's Congress to strengthen patent protection for pharmaceuticals. And in Brazil, a government-appointed commission drew up a new intellectual property code. If, as expected, other Latin American nations follow suit, the reforms could attract a wave of new investment by U.S. pharmaceutical makers that have been wary of the region.

How far have we come? Until 1990 it would have been unthinkable for a Chilean president to host a lunch for his visiting American counterpart. But since the democratically elected Aylwin came to power in March 1991, ending General Pinochet's often-repressive 16-year rule, Chile has gone from being something of a pariah in the eyes of the U.S. to a model of the democratic free-market economies. As President Bush declared, "Chile has moved farther, faster than any other nation in South America toward real free-market reform." In fact, Chile wants to be the first South American nation to negotiate a free-trade accord with the U.S. Clearly this trend toward economic integration reinforces the declining advantages of the large nation-state and the increasing gains from access to larger markets.

Significant concerns remain. Chile's recent spate of terrorist actions continue to worry many that the nation remains politically unstable, which could threaten the economic miracle. Human rights violations continue to haunt the nation. Furthermore, an estimated five million Chileans— one third of the population—still live in poverty conditions.

Contradictions exist. On the prosperity side, the inflation rate in the first third of 1991 averaged less than 6 percent, with an economic growth projected to be almost 5 percent in 1991. The savings rate is more than twice that of the United States. Foreign exchange reserves have doubled since 1990 and the stock market has nearly doubled between 1990 and 1991. Investment has been running at almost a $2 billion record annual rate.

The Phelps Dodge Corporation is building a $300 million copper mine in the north, while Australian, Spanish, and Japanese backers have poured $1 billion into Chile's copper belt to create the world's third-largest copper mine. The Simpson Paper Company of San Francisco, together with one of Chile's largest forestry companies, is building a $400 million pulp and paper plant near Concepción. Shell Oil has a plant of similar size.

President Bush on June 27, 1991 officiated at a White House ceremony with Chile's Finance Minister Alejandro Foxley, where an accord writing off $16 million in obligations Chile incurred in buying American food with federal financing was signed. Chile thus became the first country to reduce its debt to the U.S. government under Bush's plan to stimulate Latin American trade and investment. In addition, the President asked Congress to approve debt forgiveness for up to the entire $7 billion of U.S. assistance given to Latin America for food, export-financing, and other programs.

In the meantime, most Latin American nations are rushing to privatize their industries. Brazil prepared to sell off two big steel firms in 1991, Usiminas and Tubarao. Now that the Banco Occidental has been sold, a telephone company is for sale in Venezuela, along with a Caracas raceway, the national airline, and ports. Bolivia plans to privatize a stake in its airline, Lloyd Aereo Boliviano, all of its railways, and its five-star Hotel La Paz.

In Central America, activity to privatize is picking up. Honduras has already privatized 13 state enterprises for $34 million, with other companies on the block, including its banana plantation, a hotel, a steel company, two sawmills, a sugar mill, and a cheese factory. El Salvador's government is selling its Presidente Hotel in San Salvador as well as seven sugar mills and, eventually, her state-run banks. Having just concluded a cease-fire in January 1992, El Salvador will move even faster to privatize her industries.

On January 9, 1991, Mexico decided to enter into a trade zone agreement with her five impoverished nations to its south. President Salinas de Gortari hosted a two-day meeting on the subject in Tuxtla Gutierrez, Chiapas, a southern state bordering Guatemala, the first time Mexico has joined the five nations in a summit to ease the burden of war and underdevelopment on the isthmus. The agenda included a proposal for free trade from the Rio Grande to Costa Rica's border with Panama. Such an accord would be welcomed by the Central American nations in that it would guarantee greater exports to Mexico and eventually lead to more open trade with the United States. (The U.S. is Central America's largest commercial partner with two-way trade in 1989 totaling nearly $5 billion.)

The summit produced a new arrangement concerning the payment of Mexican oil and formalized the plan for a free-trade zone with the isthmus. According to the Chiapas declaration, as the mid-January meeting is popularly referred to, the President's commitment to a free-trade zone is scheduled for the end of 1996, and may possibly extend to Colombia and Venezuela. This will be accomplished through a gradual reduction of tariffs, accompanied by measures to eliminate domestic subsidies and other unfair practices. Mexico's tariffs top off at about 20 percent, compared with a 40 percent average top rate in Central America, a substantial difference that should cushion the shock of competition for protected industries.

Presently, Central American imports from Mexico consist mostly of oil, and exports to that nation are largely foodstuffs and some finished products. For example, Costa Rica imported $100 million of goods in 1990, half of its oil, and exported to Mexico only $15 million worth, a third of which were food products.

Central American countries would like to expand their open export markets north of Mexico and significantly reach the U.S. and Canadian consumers. This will come slowly, and the first step for these isthmus nations may well demand establishing a track record first with Mexico. They will also have to manipulate the growing pie as other larger nations in South America, many of whom also have framework agreements with Washington, demand closer trade relations. Queuing up, along with patience, may well be the characteristics needed for negotiation.

Nevertheless, Mexican trade with Central American nations has been impressive and profitable. It was $500 million in 1989, just 1.1 percent of the nation's total import-export bill. But the region's farm exports and sales of raw materials to Mexico would soar if U.S. firms flock to Mexico under the free-trade accord between the two nations. Increased trade between Mexico and Central America would deflect criticism in Mexico that her government had turned its back on Latin America while forging closer ties with the United States.

Mexico has become the window of opportunity for Central America. With her remarkable transformation, Mexico is having a positive influence on the nations south of its borders. Central American countries seek Mexico's advice and cooperation in their own transitions to more open economies.

As if to prepare for a successful Mexico-U.S.-Canada free-trade zone, the five chiefs of states of Central America met in San Salvador on July 15, 1991 to plan the region's future. Their new strategy is to get a slice of the hemisphere's booming free-trade activity by negotiating bloc trade accords with the U.S. and other nations. A careful watch is kept on Mexico's maquiladora business. As wages increase along the U.S.-Mexican border some of these so-called screwdriver plants have already moved to Guatemala and Honduras, where wages are even lower. Central American officials would like Mexico to prosper but want their nations to attract still more of these U.S. exported subsidiaries.

No one is entering these Latin American relationships with tainted eyes. There remains a long way to go. Latin American economies remain layered with restrictions built up during decades of static policies pursued by military and civilian governments alike. In addition, U.S. protectionist lobbies continue to place a brake on future negotiations.

As civilian-controlled governments replaced military-controlled governments throughout Latin America, their armies had to find new things to do as their budgets kept shrinking. Today, military men are scrambling to find useful work to defend their budgetary requests. Their army engineers are concentrating on the building of roads, schools, and bridges; they are preparing the infrastructure for agrarian reform settlements.

For example, in Argentina, the number of army conscripts has fallen from a traditional level of 50,000 a year to about 10,000. Where military-owned firms produce petrochemicals, iron ore, and light arms, among other things, their Congress is privatizing 21 of these businesses—about half. In a period far shorter than that of Mexico, Argentina has already sold its telephone company, its state airline, television and radio stations, and four petrochemical plants. It has leased 6,200 miles of roads and 3,100 miles of railway lines. A repair dockyard, more railway leases, two chemical firms, and concessions for ten marginal oilfields were sold in 1991. Toward the end of the year the government sold concessions to run the electricity, water, and gas companies serving Buenos Aires along with some harbors, four established oilfields, and the National Mint. And still later, Argentina plans to sell outright their state shipping line, ELMA.

The population of the seven Central American nations (Belize, Costa Rica, El Salvador, Guatemala, Honduras, Nicaragua, and Panama) approached 28,000,000 in 1990, with a similar census for the Caribbean nations. Thirteen nations of South America (Argentina, Bolivia, Brazil, Chile, Colombia, Ecuador, French Guiana, Guyana, Paraguay, Peru, Suriname, Uruguay, and Venezuela) combine to add approximately 280,000,000 people who represent an ever increasing and demanding consumer force.

Unfortunately, 180 million Latin Americans, 50 million more than in 1982, are living in poverty. Sixty percent of the population earn less than 18 percent of the total income and are undernourished, underemployed, undereducated, and underpaid. It is estimated that 30 years or more will be needed to lift the poorest 20 percent of Latin Americans out of poverty.

Health, food problems, and education need to be addressed. Shockingly, more infants died in Latin America than were born in Europe, a sobering commentary on underdevelopment. In El Salvador, three out of every four children are undernourished; in Bolivia, one out of every three infants dies during the first year of life. The overall illiteracy rate still hovers at 40 percent.

Adding to the existing burdens are untreated waste and inadequate drinking water facilities which as spreaders of the deadly cholera exacerbate health problems. Preying on many Latin American nations, cholera will weaken these already shaky economies. For example, in the winter of 1991, a wave of barriers flew up around the world to block Peru's food exports, where more than one-thousand people died of cholera (the last major U.S. cholera epidemic was in 1866). Tourism in Peru declined by nearly three-quarters. Forty percent of Lima's 7 million residents do not have access to potable, piped water; 40 percent of Brazil's 150 million people do not have access to sewers. Any free-trade agreement will hang in balance until funds are provided to build latrines and to install water purification units and water tanks which are needed to eliminate this killer.

Deteriorating conditions in Brazil, by the end of 1991, created a pessimism throughout the country. Brazilians watched their currency lose 1 percent of its value daily. The country finished the year as Latin America's only nation with a rising, triple-digit annual inflation rate. Further aggravating life, salaries shrank by 20 percent, with prices climbing by 26 percent. Economic disarray and the potential for unrest in the streets of Brazil are being tempted.

In addition, aggregate foreign debt is $410 billion, (the third world's largest debtor, Brazil, owes $123 billion), nearly $100 billion more than in 1982, and requires a net annual outflow in interest and principal payments of about $25 billion—or more than 20 percent of Latin American exports. The work force grows at a faster rate than the creation of new jobs. The annual per capita income remains low, about one-tenth that of the United States. In the mid-1980s, per capita income dropped 10 percent in Latin America.

Open-market reforms will be needed. For example, Brazil has import tariffs that average 35.6 percent and range up to 85 percent as its president dropped import bans on more than 1,000 products in July 1990. He also vowed to lower import tariffs from an average of 80 percent to 20 percent by 1994. In Venezuela, the average is 27.59 percent and the maximum, 100 percent. In Colombia, the average is 26.69 percent and the maximum is 200 percent. Argentina reduced its maximum import tariff to 39 percent and the average is down to 18.22 percent.

Despite her hyperinflation (although her monthly rate was down to 2.6 percent in July 1991), budget deficits, and frequent currency reforms, Argentina is certainly on the move. The government is selling ten-year concessions to run Buenos Aires's subway and suburban overground railroads. Argentina is third among the privatizers of Latin America following Chile and Mexico by having already sold its telephone company, state air-line, two TV stations, oil and gas concessions, 6,200 miles of road-maintenance projects, and the railway that takes grain to the port of Bahia Blanca. By mid-1991 her government had raised approximately $8.5 billion and projects to raise another $1.7 billion by June of 1992 by offering a steel mill and the capital's electricity firm and waterworks, to be followed by natural gas, petrochemicals, a shipping line, and several banks.

To prepare the Latin American countries for the New American Community requires building a new society in which these nations are masters of their own destiny, thereby substituting newer institutions for those discredited inheritances of the past. Latin American industries are protected from competition by a labyrinth of hidden subsidies, monopoly rights, corrupt state contracts, and outright prohibition of imports.

Changes in Latin America may come slowly. History cannot be easily erased, as shameful as it may be. Some advances only cover the truth that these nations continue to be victimized by their past. Modern advances of recent decades have provided little for the majority of people.

Economies in Latin American states grow but fail to develop, and institutions of former years continue to hold a grip on keeping the living standard low.

Nowhere is the potential for change so evident than in Central and South America, where poor people live in rich lands. So much of the solution must come from within, with new or reordered values. The power base must shift away from the few to the greater number. The privileges of the elite must be shared for the welfare of the many to improve. Land ownership must be spread beyond the powerful; unemployment must be reduced with massive public projects and all welfare benefits must be made available for everyone. The symptoms of a classic underdeveloped region are ever present: high birth and death rates, illiteracy, undernourishment, low per capita income, unequal distribution of wealth, and trade dependency. The enigma can be massaged in different ways. One part of the puzzle, demanding solution, must be economic.

An example from Peru portends great future possibilities for this struggling nation and for others in Latin America. One of their leading economists, Hernando de Soto, concluded after conducting research in Peruvian slums, that the shackles of mercantilism and state control that has limited individual achievement and competition throughout Latin America has a tremendously large informal economic sector.

In the spring of 1991, Peruvian President Alberto Fujimori (Latin America's first president of Japanese descent) slashed the three import tariff rates to only two: 15 percent and 25 percent. All pending permits and paperwork requirements affecting foreign trade were eliminated. Steps were taken to liberalize the flow of capital in and out of Peru, making it possible for the first time in decades to allow Peruvians to freely keep bank accounts anywhere in the world and hold international credit cards without breaking the law. The state monopoly in reinsurance and the privileges of the state insurance company were eliminated and foreign investment laws and laws regarding the labor market were liberalized.

Unfortunately though, typical of Central and South American nations, many businesspeople in Peru work in the black market as a means of bypassing the elitist, protected private sector that serves as the official economy. In the informal massive sector, people are judged not by who they know, but by what they have produced. In most cases however, they operate without the security of property rights and consequently, their gains could be easily confiscated at will.

By successfully fighting the Peruvian government, Mr. Soto addressed the need to secure greater property rights to permit the informal sector to operate above ground, thereby allowing a growing middle-class population able to support itself and contribute to the betterment of society. Within a six month period in 1991, 30,000 properties were registered to arouse the freedom of previously concealed business activities. The reg-

istry program for individuals with property claims, along with easier procedures for incorporating which previously took nearly one year and now
can be accomplished in one day (6,000 new enterprises were registered
in three months), is a booming success. Peru is making strides to lift itself
into a constructive procedure for raising the nation's standard of living
by providing a healthier opportunity for the expansion of business.

President Fujimori reduced Peru's monthly inflation rate to 8 percent
in March 1991, from 62 percent when he assumed office in July of 1990.
At the same time, the highest tariffs on imports were cut to 25 percent
from 50 percent, and tariffs now average 17 percent, the lowest level in
Peruvian history.

Impressed by her free-market economic strategy, 15 countries, meeting
in Paris in mid-May 1991 attempted to raise $360 million to assist Peru in
repaying its overdue interest with the multilateral bank. This impressive
model should spread throughout the hemisphere.

There was an incredible surge of dollar deposits in Peruvian banks by
mid-1991, some $600–$700 million, which was equivalent to Peru's net
international reserves, or half its annual revenue from mineral exports.
This minor miracle followed 20 years of corrupt government, in excess
of three years of significant recession, and an inflation rate each month
of between 8 and 30 percent.

President Alberto Fujimori was on the move. He started to sell shares
in state firms, lowered tariffs, doubled tax collections from a low of 4
percent of GDP to nearly 8 percent, and had liberated interest rates.
Significantly, a framework agreement was signed with the United States
on "eradicating or substituting" the Peruvian coca crop that supplies more
than half the world's raw material for cocaine.

Landlocked Bolivia has also been a pacesetter for South America. Bolivia was the first nation to present a specific proposal on reduction of
her bilateral debt with the U.S. On the trade front, Bolivia has reduced
tariffs to the point where they are the lowest in South America, and is
steering the Andean Pact toward a Free Trade Agreement by 1992.

In the mid-1980s Bolivia faced a 25,000 percent inflation rate. By 1990
her inflation was the lowest in South America. All of her non-tariff barriers
were lifted and import duties were reduced to a maximum of 10 percent
for all goods and a maximum of 5 percent for capital equipment, the main
U.S. export to Bolivia. Bolivia has become a model of reform among her
neighbors. The speed of negotiations toward a freer economy is impressive. In December 1991 five Andean nations agreed to form a free-trade
zone and a customs union effective January 1992. This was the most
important agreement of the 22-year-old Andean Trade Pact where the
customs union set similar tariffs for goods and services imports in 1992,
three years earlier than originally planned for Peru, Bolivia, Colombia,
Ecuador, and Venezuela. The free-trade zone eliminating taxes also began

on the same date for Bolivia, Colombia, and Venezuela, and six months later for Ecuador and Peru.

At present, perhaps Chile or maybe Colombia, whose living standards have risen in the last decade, is the nearest Latin American nation prepared to enter into free-trade negotiation with the New American Community. If so, then either or both could well become the model for others.

There remains the light of optimism. With its abundance of natural resources and ample labor, there is much potential for Latin America. Its land area is more than twice the size of Europe's, with a population smaller than Europe's. It occupies 19 percent of the globe's terrain but contains only 7 percent of the world's population.

Once again, it would be foolhardy to anticipate a rapid hemispheric embracing of the New American Community. The realities of all regions point to political, economic, and social obstacles that will demand tireless effort and understanding before corrections can be made for a true infusion of trust and cooperation. Patience, the code for future hope and opportunity, must constantly be on the list of frustrated people who can rapidly turn away from the trials of apparent futility. But, the continuing search for a final goal that purports to lift a large segment of the world to greater heights and living standards demands a determination not to surrender, no matter what the odds.

The balancing act will certainly require the crawl prior to the step, and clearly before the long run. First in place, we must evolve an economic union of free-trade accords between the United States, Canada, and Mexico. This will, with mounting success across borders, lead to further social and political overtures and agreements. As these phases move forward, concurrent attempts at diplomacy and negotiation should introduce prospects for independent free-trade agreements between any of the three founding members of the NAC and other Latin American neighbors, or pursued in a parallel effort by the central administration of the NAC. In any case, all sides should encourage and support those nations interested in joining the partnership of the New American Community.

While the Latin American Free Trade Association and a Central American Common Market failed, the movement is quickening with a new bright economic scheme. On March 26, 1991, meeting in Asunción, the Paraguayan capital, the presidents of Brazil, Argentina, Uruguay, and Paraguay signed a treaty creating a common Latin American trading market. The Southern Cone Common Market treaty, known as Mercosur or the Treaty of Asunción (Paraguay) was modeled on the European Community's 1957 Treaty of Rome. With headquarters in Montevideo, Uruguay, it will dismantle trade barriers and encourage cross-border investment and joint projects over the coming four years. Beginning January 1, 1995 there will be no tariffs on trade between the four South American neighbors.

The plan is to create a market of 190 million people, accounting for more than half the gross domestic product of Latin America and the Caribbean. Until then, tariffs are scheduled to drop gradually, as will restrictions on the movement of goods, services, capital, and labor. Progress is being made with high expectations. What took 35 years in Europe to accomplish, the presidents of these nations are attempting in less than four years.

The challenge is severe, as inflation differs widely. Brazil's rate in 1990 was 1,800 percent, Argentina's 1,344 percent, Uruguay's 129 percent, and Paraguay's about 40 percent. The United States negotiated the framework for a free-trade agreement with the four nations. By year's end 1994 these four nations will have formed a common market, housing 190 million people, and accounting for more than half the output of Latin America and the Caribbean. When taken as a whole, Latin America (Argentina, Bolivia, Brazil, Chile, Colombia, Costa Rica, Ecuador, Guatemala, Mexico, Peru, Uruguay, and Venezuela) remains an attractive source of investment.

By mid-summer of 1991, a growing number of Latin American economists and U.S. free-trade supporters called for increased leadership on inter-American trade issues. Specifically, there was a growing demand to create a U.S.-based organization, working closely with Latin American nations to promote unrestricted hemispheric commerce, to serve as:

1. a clearinghouse, to collect, systematize, and disseminate trade statistics and information on national trade policies;
2. a think tank, to analyze trade and trade-related issues;
3. a trade monitor, to review and evaluate proposed trade arrangements among nations; and
4. a source of technical assistance, to provide expertise to countries formulating trade policies and negotiating trade agreements.

It was suggested that in time, such a hemispheric trade organization would be entrusted with the more sensitive tasks of defining rules to guide hemispheric trade negotiations, mediating them, investigating alleged violations of trade accords, and settling disputes.

This is but the beginning. As Rudiger Dornbusch of the Massachusetts Institute of Technology wrote in *The Economist*,

The free-trade agreement represents a foreign policy commitment to political stability and prosperity in the region. Greater stability is based on economic prosperity and political freedom. Just as on the economic front, nothing works better to open up a country's political system than exposing it to trade. The European Community brought Spain, Greece and Portugal into the fold, stabilizing them economically and politically. North American free trade, likewise, is designed to bring political openness to Mexico and to begin the economic and political rehabilitation that Central and South America need.

As the year 1991 ended, and the European Community's grand scheme for 1992 approached, a close look at the economic landscape of Latin America indicated a dramatic movement away from the past. The decade of crippling inflation, no growth, increased foreign debt, protectionism, and weighty subsidized government payrolls and budgets is moving toward being balanced and privatization of state properties represent the new symbol for growth.

Free markets, open economies, and deregulation are becoming commonplace south of the U.S. border. The optimism reached a new high when the International Monetary Fund, the International Bank for Development, and the United Nations cautiously predicted a new Latin America era of "vigorous, though sporadic, economic growth."

Once in place, a 33-nation economic, trade, political, and social bloc will stretch from Anchorage, Alaska to Patagonia, Chile. By then, this sleeping giant of 700 million people—the ultimate New American Community—will have awakened and responded in excellent fashion to another significant challenge in a splendid history.

7

THE NEW AMERICAN COMMUNITY TREATY*

PREAMBLE

Whereas, liberation of the people can best be achieved by liberation of the market economy;

Whereas, the market system can do more than any other system yet known to improve human welfare;

Whereas, all must endeavor to attain both the humanistic and social goals and productive power of an economic system based on individual effort and competition;

Whereas, the need exists to reconcile economic growth with moral concern for fellow men and women and human cost;

Whereas, there is a demand for a competitive market economy with social development programs designed to provide economic opportunities for all;

Whereas, market-distorting price controls, often adopted to help the less fortunate, have negative economic and social consequences;

*These major proposed concepts for The New American Community Treaty, appear as *Articles*. The primary model for this treaty is the original European Community Treaty and its subsequent Single European Act.

Whereas, the responsibility of the nation is to develop human resources for both economic and social ends, especially in the fields of health, education, and the strengthening of community and family, but not with permanent dependency;

Whereas, the need exists to improve productivity, but also to reduce the cost of labor, including benefits and a virtually guaranteed lifetime employment;

Whereas, concentrated production impedes the free flow of goods and services;

Whereas, a relatively strong and stable currency and banking system is required;

Whereas, foreign investors must be protected against arbitrary confiscation of their assets;

Whereas, the Latin American system must shift from a mercantilist approach, where the nation has been captured by special-interest groups from bureaucrats and business and labor people, to a capitalist system;

Whereas, solidarity should be developed within the context of a free, competitive and flexible economy, with a less interventionist and regulatory nation, creating instead the policy environment for economic success, while channeling budgetary resources to assist the less fortunate;

Whereas, the need exists for an institutional structure to inspire solidarity and charity in individual economic decision-making;

Whereas, there must be a ban in the export of hazardous wastes, a reduction in air and water pollution, and the fulfillment of internationally recognized environmental standards;

Whereas, full unification implies a political bond able to minimize separate nationalistic attitudes, thus enabling all to speak and act as one;

Be It Resolved, these goals can be achieved by cooperative efforts and genuine aspirations of inspired leaders and citizens in the development of a New American Community, in a framework that protects private contracts, provides for currency convertibility, encourages the development of free trade in a private enterprise system, protects the social and human rights of all, and provides the voice of political unity.

THE TREATY

Article 1—Objectives of the New American Community

The Community shall have as its task, by establishing a common market and progressively bringing together the economic policies of member nations, to promote throughout the NAC a harmonious development of economic activities, a continuous and balanced expansion, an increase in stability, an accelerated raising of the standard of living, and closer relations among the countries belonging to it.

Article 2—Activities of the New American Community

To achieve the objectives of the New American Community, activities shall include, as provided in this Treaty:

1. the elimination of custom duties and of quantitative restrictions on the import and export of goods among member nations, and of all other measures having equivalent effect;
2. the establishment of a common customs tariff and of a common commercial policy toward nations outside the New American Community;
3. the abolition of obstacles to freedom of movement for persons, services, and capital among the member nations;
4. the adoption of common and coordinated policies in the spheres of agriculture, transport, health, education, monetary, research, and standards;
5. the institution of a system ensuring that competition in the common market is not distorted;
6. the application of procedures by which the economic policies of member nations can be coordinated and disequilibria in their internal and external balance of payments remedied;
7. the development of a common set of laws of member nations to the extent required for the proper functioning of the common market;
8. the creation and funding of a New American Community Social Fund in order to improve employment opportunities for workers and to contribute to the raising of their standard of living;
9. the establishment of a New American Community Investment Bank to facilitate the economic expansion of the Community by opening up fresh resources;
10. the association of overseas nations and territories in order to increase trade and to promote jointly economic and social development.

Article 3—Non-Discrimination

Within the scope of application of this Treaty, and without prejudice to any special provisions contained therein, any discrimination against people, goods, and/or services on the grounds of nationality shall be prohibited.

Article 4—Internal Market

The New American Community shall adopt measures with the aim of fostering and eventually establishing the internal market which shall comprise an area without internal economic borders in which the free movements of goods, persons, services, and capital is ensured in accordance with the provision of this Treaty.

Article 5—Free Movement of Goods

The New American Community shall be based upon a customs union which shall cover all trade in goods and which shall involve the prohibition between member nations of customs duties on imports and exports and of all charges having equivalent effect among member nations, and the adoption of a common customs tariff in their relations with countries that are not members.

Article 6—The Elimination of Quantitative Restrictions

Quantitative restrictions on imports and all measures having equivalent effect shall, without prejudice to the following provisions, be prohibited among member nations.

Article 7—Exception

The provisions shall not preclude prohibitions or restrictions on imports, exports, or goods in transit justified on grounds of public morality, public policy, or public security; the protection of health and life of humans, animals, or plants; the protection of national treasures possessing artistic, historic, or archeological value; or the protection of industrial or commercial property. Such prohibitions or restrictions shall not, however, constitute a means of arbitrary discrimination or a disguised restriction on trade among member nations.

Article 8—Free Movement of Persons

1. Freedom of movement for workers shall be secured within the New American Community by the end of the transition period at the latest.
2. Such freedom of movement shall entail the abolition of any discrimination in terms of employment, remuneration, and other conditions of work based on nationality among workers of the member nations.

Article 9—Right of Establishment

Companies or firms formed in accordance with the laws of a New American Community and having their registered office, central administration, or principal place of business within the Community shall be treated in the same way as natural persons of member countries.

Article 10—Services

Restrictions on freedom to provide services within the New American Community shall be progressively abolished during the transitional period. Nationals of member nations who are established in a nation of the New American Community will be free to render services in any member country.

The Council may, acting unanimously on a proposal from its Commission, extend the provision to nationals of a third country who provide services and who are established within the New American Community.

Article 11—Rules of Competition

1. The following shall be prohibited as incompatible with the common market: all agreements among undertakings, decisions by associations of undertakings and concerted practices which may affect trade among member nations and which have as their object the prevention, restriction, or distortion of competition within the common market, and in particular those which:
   a. directly or indirectly fix purchase or selling prices or any other trading conditions;
   b. limit or control production markets, technical development, or investment;
   c. share markets or sources of supply;
   d. apply dissimilar conditions to equivalent transactions with other trading parties, thereby placing them at a competitive disadvantage;
   e. making the conclusion of contracts subject to acceptance by the other parties of supplementary obligations which, by their nature or according to commercial usage, have no connection with the subject of such contracts.
2. Any agreements or decision prohibited pursuant to this Article shall be automatically void.
3. The provisions of paragraph 1 may, however, be declared inapplicable in the case of:
   a. any agreement or category of agreements between undertakings;
   b. any decision or category of decisions by associations of undertakings;

c. any concerted practice or category of concerted practices which contributes to improving the production or distribution of goods or to promoting technical or economic progress, while allowing consumers a fair share of the resulting benefit which does not:
  i. impose on the undertakings concerned restrictions which are not indispensable to the attainment of these objectives;
  ii. afford such undertakings the possibility of eliminating competition in respect to a substantial part of the products in question.

Article 12—Abuses

Any abuse by one or more undertakings of a dominant position within the common market or in a substantial part of it shall be prohibited as incompatible with the common market in so far as it may affect trade among member nations.

Such abuse may, in particular, consist in:

1. directly or indirectly imposing unfair purchase or selling prices or other unfair trading conditions;
2. limiting production, markets, or technical development to the prejudice of consumers;
3. applying dissimilar conditions to equivalent transactions with other trading parties, thereby placing them at a competitive disadvantage;
4. making the conclusion of contracts subject to acceptance by the other parties of supplementary obligations which, by their nature or according to commercial usage, have no connection with the subject of such contracts.

Article 13—Undertakings

1. In the case of public undertakings and undertakings to which member nations grant special or exclusive rights, member nations shall neither enact nor maintain in force any measure contrary to the rules contained in this Treaty.
2. Undertakings entrusted with the operation of services of general economic interest or having the character of a revenue producing monopoly shall be subject to the rules contained in this Treaty, in particular to the rules on competition, in so far as the application of such rules does not obstruct the performance, in law or fact, of the particular tasks assigned to them. The development of trade must not be affected to such an extent as would be contrary to the interests of the New American Community.
3. The Commission shall ensure the application of the provisions of this Article and shall, where necessary, address appropriate directives or decisions to member nations.

Article 14—Aid

1. Save as otherwise provided in this Treaty, any aid granted by a member nation or through national resources in any form whatsoever which distorts or threat-

ens to distort competition by favoring certain undertakings or the production of certain goods shall, insofar as it affects trade among member nations, be incompatible with the common market.

2. The Commission shall, in cooperation with member nations, keep under constant review all systems of aid existing in those nations. It shall propose to the latter any appropriate measures required by the progressive development or by the functioning of the common market.

Article 15–Approximation of Laws

1. The Council shall, acting by a qualified majority of the proposal from the Commission in cooperation with the New American Community Parliament—its legislative body—and the Economic and Social Committee, adopt the measures for the approximation of the provisions laid down by law, regulation, or administrative action in member nations which have as their object the establishment and functioning of the unified market.
2. Paragraph 1 shall not apply to fiscal provisions, to those relating to the free movement of persons, or to those relating to the rights and interests of employed persons. In such matters, unanimity shall be required.
3. The Commission, in its proposals laid down in Paragraph 1, concerning health, safety, environmental and consumer protection, will take as a base a high level of protection.
4. If, after the adoption of a standardization measure by the Council acting by a qualified majority, a member nation deems it necessary to apply national provisions, on grounds of major need, or relating to protection of the environment or the working environment, it shall notify the Commission of these provisions.

The Commission shall confirm the provisions involved after having been verified that they are not a means of arbitrary discrimination or a disguised restriction on trade between member nations.

By way of derogation from procedures, the Commission or any member nation may bring the matter directly before the Court of Justice if it considers that another New American Community country is making improper use of the powers provided for in this Article.

The standardization measures referred to above shall, in appropriate cases, include a safeguard clause authorizing the member nation to take, for one or more of the non-economic reasons, provisional measures subject to a New American Community control procedure.

Article 16—Enforcement Provision

Decisions of the Council or of the Commission which impose a pecuniary obligation on persons rather than nations shall be enforceable.

Enforcement shall be governed by the rules of civil procedure in force in the country in the territory of which it is carried out. The order for its enforcement shall be appended to the decision, without formality other than verification of the authenticity of the decision, by the national authority which the government of each New American Community country shall designate for this purpose and shall make known to the Commission and to the Court of Justice.

When these formalities have been completed on application by the party concerned, the latter may proceed to enforcement in accordance with the national law, by bringing the matter directly before the competent authority.

Enforcement may be suspended only by a decision of the Court of Justice. However, the courts of the country concerned shall have jurisdiction over complaints that enforcement is being carried out in an irregular manner.

* * *

The foundation and support for the New American Community rests with its Treaty, this one or another preferred one, negotiated by founding members. By design it should be general and brief, allowing the exceptional issue to be dealt with later, thereby not restricting future opportunities by minimizing flexibility or attending to a larger audience of situation and need. The Treaty must command more attention than any other structural or legislative detail, for challenges, which are sure to come, must provide the various pressure groups and the Court of Justice with ample clarity for interpretation. Amendments will flow, as they should, but the Treaty, the NAC Constitution, should remain as the guiding principle for continuity, determination, and to provide a heritage worthy of its efforts.

8

STRUCTURE OF THE NEW AMERICAN COMMUNITY

Once North American free-trade accords are signed, the New American Community Treaty can be negotiated based on the free-trade agreements that would be the seed for designing a critical structure as its foundation for all future endeavors. This Treaty would lay out the framework for a North American agreement, that would, with the passage of time and cooperation, be expanded to incorporate different nations of Central and South America, with island nations of the Caribbean, thereby creating a 33-nation trade bloc.

Initially, the mandate for the NAC would emanate from the nations to the north, the United States, Canada, and Mexico, which with its combined populations of more than 350 million and GNP exceeding $6 trillion annually is a core for experimentation and a center for creation. Once in place, others will be invited to join.

The model for an NAC structure might come from the European Community, one that has been studied, tried, and revised numerous times. Aside from the fact that North America shares many of Western Europe's hopes and aspirations for the future, we are privileged to have watched and assessed the nearly 35 years of evolution going from its 1957 Treaty of Rome and its fundamental creation, to a projected single market for 12 member states at the close of 1992.

While not all E.C. tests and experiences have been successful (or are applicable to the NAC), while ocean differences urge caution in adapting their regulations and structure, while the world changes necessitate new strategies indicating that not all is efficient, it would also be foolhardy to discard the model without sound reason, for decades of insight can save the NAC considerable time, money, debate, and most importantly, poor judgment. By borrowing from the E.C., we not only flatter them by emulation, but provide that a tested format has considerable merit in our thrust forward.

The description in Figure 2, though based on the E.C. organization, incorporates pragmatic indulgencies that draw on the multitude of differences, not only from the 12 member states of the European Community, but more importantly, reflect the unique, wonderful and at the same time problematic entities separating the three founding nations. Certainly, this design must someday extend to all of the Americas.

COUNTERBALANCING FORCES

A Treaty, first prepared and signed by the governments of Mexico, Canada, and the U.S. would firmly and with pride establish the New American Community with its branch institutions to manage its future, conscience, decision-making, and prosperity. It would be structured to include: an executive branch that might be called the *Commission*; a major decision-making unit that might be called the *Council of Ministers*; a representative and advisory unit with balancing powers over the Council and Commission that might be called the *Parliament*; an advisory group of special interest organizations dealing with recommendation for policy and proposals that might be called the *Economic and Social Committee*; throughout an independent high court that might be called the *Court of Justice*; an independent budgetary office to examine the accounts, revenues, and expenditures of the NAC institutions that might be called the *Court of Auditors*; an investment financial institution that would raise funds on the capital markets and grant loans and loan guarantees on a non-profit basis to facilitate the financing of NAC projects that might be called the *New American Community Investment Bank*. Once these institutions are in place, other institutions can follow as amendments to the New American Community Treaty.

The Commission

An alternative name would be the "Executive Branch" of the NAC, and in several ways it would be the most important unit. Its purpose would be to ensure the proper functioning of the NAC, and it is the institution that should represent the interests of the NAC as a whole. To this end, the *Commission* will initiate NAC legislation, ensure participating nations' compliance with the Treaty, and legislate on its own in areas where this power is delegated to it by the *Council*. In its role as drafter of NAC legislation, it is probably the most important of the NAC

Figure 2

THE NEW AMERICAN COMMUNITY LEGISLATIVE PROCESS

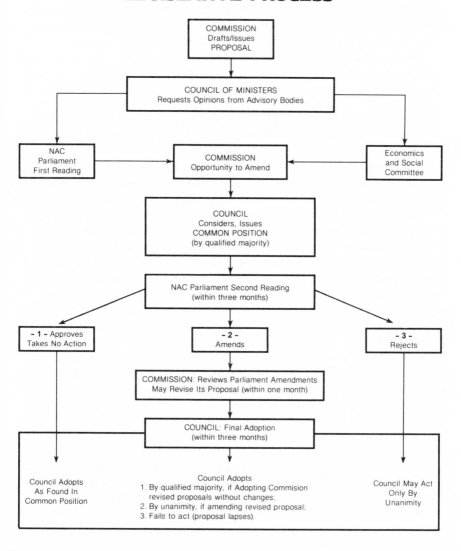

institutions for business. It is here that NAC legislation and policies will be monitored or affected as they are being molded.

Composition. The *Commission* will be composed of commissioners including one president and six commissioners (or vice-presidents) at the outset (within the North American Community). Each commissioner will be assigned a portfolio, with responsibility for one or more substantive areas dealt with by the directorates-general (DG).

Each commissioner will be appointed for a four-year renewable term by mutual agreement of the governments of NAC nations. The president is appointed for a two-year renewable term.

There will be commissioners from each of the NAC nations, the number determined by the size of the population of the participating nation, with a maximum of two for the largest and one for the smaller populated nations. All commissioners will be required to act independently of their governments and of the Council of Ministers. Overall political control will be exercised by the Parliament, which shall be able to dismiss the Commission, or any of its commissioners, as a whole.

Directorates-General. The bulk of the Commission's work, including the drafting of proposals for NAC legislation, will be done by directorates-general (DGs), each responsible for specific substantive areas.

The top posts in each directorate-general (the director-general, directors, and heads of division) are to be appointed by collective agreement among the commissioners. There should be an informal agreement that a rough balance will be maintained among the different nationalities when making these appointments, and that certain posts will be held by particular nations, but this should be flexible.

In addition, the Commission should have a secretariat-general to organize the work of the Commission, and a legal service to advise on legal matters in the formulation of legislation and policy in the Commission.

Cabinets. Each commissioner will be assisted by a "Cabinet" to play a key role as a liaison between the commissioners, the directorates-general, and other interests. The Cabinet will be staffed by 6–8 people handpicked by the commissioner and headed by a chef-de-cabinet, who often will represent the commissioner in his/her absence. Agreements reached here may only need formal approval by the Commission.

Powers and Responsibilities: to draft legislation. The Commission shall have the exclusive authority to initiate NAC legislation. However, it can and does initial proposals in response to calls from the Council or the Parliament. It is therefore in the Commission that NAC legislation and policies that affect business are to be formulated.

To take decisions and adopt legislation on its own to implement NAC policies, where the Council has delegated to it this authority. A particularly pertinent example for firms is competition policy, where the Commission should conduct investigations and impose fines on companies which it believes are violating the NAC's rules banning anti-competititive practices. Another example is anti-dumping policy, where the Commission should investigate and fine firms from other nations, in order to implement policies of the NAC.

To ensure the enforcement of the Treaties. The Commission shall issue a "reasoned opinion" to any NAC nation that has not complied with an obligation under the Treaties, and bring the nation before the Court of Justice if it fails to heed the Commission's opinion.

To negotiate international trade agreements with third nations on behalf of the NAC. For example, the Commission will negotiate on the NAC's behalf in the General Agreement on Tariffs and Trade meetings. Negotiations should be authorized and supervised, and the agreements ratified, by the Council.

To manage the funds and common policies which will constitute the bulk of the NAC's budget. For example, funding for poorer regions of the NAC.

Voting. The Commission will serve as a collegial body with collective responsibility for its actions. The Commission will approve proposals by a simple majority vote, although a commissioner should be able to delay a proposal.

Functioning. The Commission staff will grow with need, with the majority of its staff centered in a location of one country but not the same nation as for other primary institutions of the New American Community. One of its responsibilities will be providing linguistic/translation services in the languages of the NAC. Proposals for legislation should be drafted by staff in the DGs, but must be approved by the Commission itself before being issued as formal Commission proposals for consideration by the Council of Ministers and Parliament. The commissioners will meet once a week on a specified day; the meetings will be chaired by the president. The chefs-de-cabinet should meet at least two days earlier to prepare for the commissioner's meeting. Where the Cabinets reach agreement on a proposal, the Commission may issue it without discussion.

Access. In drafting proposals, directorates-general will usually consult the other institutions and outside interests. Although there is to be no formal or systematic procedure for the submission of comments to the Commission as it is drafting or revising legislation, written comments can be submitted by interested parties informally at any time to the appropriate Commission officials in the directorates-general, or the commissioner and his/her cabinet. The commissioner may also decide to solicit the views of interested parties.

Usually, the Commission officials will be receptive to expert input from firms, both NAC and non-NAC, when provided in a way that is useful to them. This will be true for several reasons, but primarily because of the complexities of the issues and the relatively small size of the NAC staff. Therefore it will be particularly important for drafters to hear from recognized experts and for staffers to maintain close liaison with appropriate parties involved in debate.

The Council of Ministers

The *Council of Ministers* will be the principal decision-making body of the NAC and should decide on legislative proposals emanating from the Commission. Composed of ministerial-level representatives from each of the national governments in the NAC, the Council is the institution where the interests of the nations are represented, although they are to make decisions with the aim of ensuring the attainment of the objectives of the NAC Treaties.

Composition. The Council will be composed of ministerial-level representatives from the nations of the NAC. Different ministers meet, depending on the subject being addressed (e.g., the Council of Agricultural Ministers, on agricultural matters). The presidency of the Council of Ministers will be rotated among the NAC nations on an alphabetical basis, based on the spelling in their own languages with a term of office for six months, from January to June and from July to December of each year.

Powers and Responsibilities: to make decisions that are legally binding (final adoption of proposed regulations, directives, or decisions); to promote the coordination of NAC nations' economic policies; to make proposals to the Commission for initiatives that should contribute to the NAC's objectives.

Voting. Each decision made by the Council of Ministers will be founded on a proposal by the Commission, and will be made by qualified majority on matters pertaining to the completion of an internal common market within the NAC. On fiscal matters, those relating to the free movement of persons or to those relating to the rights and interests of employed persons, a unanimous vote will be required and nations within the NAC will still have the authority to veto proposed legislation. (This necessitates under a situation where unanimity is called for that it be achieved ultimately, or that the nation(s) resisting the will of the vast majority change to support this expression or withdraw or be asked to resign from the New American Community). This should be considered the very last course of action, with reentry by the removed country being automatic once acceptance of the vote has been accomplished. A qualified majority is determined by a system of weighted voting, and would require a 2/3 vote for passage. The nations with the combined largest population and GNP will receive the most votes, and in descending order the number of privileged votes will decline on a graduated scale from 10, to 8, to 4, to 2 votes.

In actuality, greater use of qualified majority voting means that the fate of any piece of proposed legislation may depend on a complicated set of alliances. A blocking minority will be needed to prevent legislation from passing, or must be avoided to see legislation passed. It suggests that legislation is adopted more rapidly. A nation, for example, that objects to a proposal is less likely to press its points if it knows it does not have the support of a blocking minority. Monitoring of NAC nations' positions is therefore more important than ever for firms interested in a given piece of legislation.

Functioning. Formal meetings of the Council of Ministers on each substantive area should be held approximately monthly. Individual proposals will be examined by working groups, composed of the relevant staff from the Council and the Committee of Regular Officials (see below), national experts, and the Commission.

The presidency sets the schedule of meetings at the beginning of its six-month term and chairs the Council meetings. It also sets the Council's priorities for its term and it will play a central role in determining what should be accomplished in this time. A statement is made by each presidency on the priorities for its term. To facilitate transitions and coordination of the Council's agenda in the longer term, the present and immediate past and future presidencies meet as a threesome.

A secretary-general, appointed by the Council, should coordinate the work of the Council and of the Committee of Regular Officials. The secretary-general will be appointed by the Council for a renewable term of five years.

Access. Once a proposal is presented by the Commission to the Council of Ministers for the Council's consideration, it becomes more difficult to follow, or influence, the measure's progress.

Council deliberations, where the interests of national governments are negotiated, are not transparent. All meetings are to be closed to the public and working texts should remain confidential. As an alternative at the outset, some public indication of Council views or the state of negotiations on a given proposal would be found in the press following ministerial meetings, statements by the presidency, and answers to parliamentary questions. Nations of the NAC would also seek the views of interested parties from their own countries, including national and NAC-wide business and industrial groups.

Committee of Regular Officials (CORO). The function of the Committee of Regular Officials will be to prepare and facilitate the work of the Council of Ministers. Each nation of the NAC will maintain an embassy to the NAC, which will be headed by a regular official with ambassadorial status.

The CORO will deal with matters of a political nature. The deputy COROs should handle matters of lesser importance, while those of a technical nature should be addressed in working groups of the appropriate specialists from the NAC nations. The chairman of CORO will be of the same nationality as the president of the Council of Ministers, and hold office for the same six-month term. CORO will supervise the working parties of the Council of Ministers and prepare the Council's advisory body meetings, in order to prepare the ground for discussion at the ministerial level. CORO will not have the power to issue formal decisions; those decisions are to be made by the Council of Ministers. However, if the officials and the Commission agree unanimously, the Council does not have to be consulted on matters of lesser importance.

THE NEW AMERICAN COMMUNITY COUNCIL (NACC)

Not to be confused with the Council of Ministers of the NAC, NACC will be composed of the heads of government of NAC nations. Its meetings will be attended by the president of the Commission, to discuss NAC affairs and foreign policy issues. Although NACC will not have any formal legislative or executive authority, NACC will play a central role in addressing important political questions that cannot be resolved at the ministerial level, and in providing political guidance to the ministers and setting the broad political agenda for the NAC. These NACC meetings should be held at least twice a year, in June and December, in the capital or designated city of the NAC nation ending its six-month term in the Council presidency.

The Parliament

The Parliament will be the major "advisory" institution of the New American Community and its most "representative" institution in that it is the only one directly elected by NAC citizens. Although its opinions are not binding, it must be consulted on most proposed NAC legislation. This power of consultation means that the Parliament can delay legislation by withholding its opinion, and that the Commission and the Council must take greater account of the Parliament's recommendations to modify or reject draft NAC legislation. Parliament should also have some budgetary powers and powers of control over the Commission and the Council of Ministers. When a void exists or given time, greater power should be placed in the hands of the elected citizens represented in the Parliament.

Composition. The Parliament should be directly elected every five years. Elections will take place in each country of the NAC. A proportional representation system should be employed in the selection of members of the Parliament. The president of Parliament should be elected by the members for a term of two-and-a-half years. Seat allocation should be determined by national population where the largest countries have the greatest representation.

Powers and Responsibilities: To deliver opinions on NAC legislation proposed by the Commission before decision by the Council of Ministers. Members of Parliament should have a right to be consulted on certain legislation before its adoption by the Council. The Parliament can hold up legislation by not issuing an opinion. In addition, the Council of Ministers should not have the power to ignore the opinions of the Parliament. The Parliament should have the right to a second reading of certain proposals, following a common position from the Council of Ministers. If at this stage the Parliament rejects a proposal, it should only be adopted by a unanimous vote in the Council. If the Parliament offers amendments, and if the Commission supports them, the Council can only reject them by a unanimous vote.

To exercise political control through: written and oral questions to the Commission and the Council. The Commission should be obliged to reply to the Parliament's questions, and the Parliament should make use of this power; dismissal of the Commission as a whole, by a two-thirds majority vote. This instrument for censure of the Commission should be employed only with the greatest reservation and thought.

To review the New American Community budget. The Parliament should be able to propose amendments to the budget, and should be able to reject the budget as a whole.

To approve all applications for NAC membership and association agreements with third world nations.

Voting. On most matters the Parliament should act by absolute majority.

Functioning. The Parliament should hold plenary sessions once a month (except either July or August) for five days when Parliament decisions will be taken. An extra session should be held in October when budgets are made and voted upon. Sessions should be open to members of the Commission and others invited to explain the Commission's position on a particular matter.

Much of the substantive work of the Parliament should be done in its committees. When a request for an Opinion of the Parliament is received from the Council on a proposal from the Commission, the Parliament will assign a lead committee to write a report, including a draft Parliament Opinion on the proposal. A person, by mutual agreement will be chosen to be in charge of drafting the committee's report. The report will then be submitted to plenary for debate and vote.

Political groups will also meet the week prior to plenary sessions.

The Secretariat should be headed by a secretary-general appointed by the Bureau. The Parliament also chooses a Bureau, which is to be entrusted with coordinating the work of the Parliament. An enlarged bureau (comprised of the president, vice-presidents, and the chairpersons of the political groups) will draw up the agenda for the plenary sessions.

The Parliament should have "interparliamentary delegations" of members which should meet with legislatures from NAC nations and non-NAC countries.

Access. Members of the Parliament are generally interested in and open to input that can assist them in the formulation of Parliament views on proposed NAC legislation. Parliament's plenary sessions should be open to the public, and the records of the sessions be made public. During the session, the minutes and untranslated debates of the previous day are to be made available daily, and should be obtainable in the same building where the sessions are being held. Beyond this, these informal records need not be publicly distributed. At a future time, however, the official and translated editions of these records should be published in an official journal.

Committee meetings, where much of the important work should be carried out, are somewhat less transparent. They may or may not be open to the public, there should be no record, permitting open and direct discussion, and committee reports should not be publicly available until following the plenary session at which they are being considered. Nonetheless, committee members and other chosen officials responsible for a report should seek pertinent information and views in their preparation.

The Economic and Social Committee

The Economic and Social Committee (ESC) should be strictly an advisory body representing employers, unions, and other special interest groups. It should be created to involve various economic and social interest groups in the NAC policy process. The ESC should express its opinion to the Council of Ministers and the Commission on many NAC proposals before they are to be adopted in their final form, but all such opinions are not to be binding, and the ESC's influence is consequently minimal and limited. Still, it should be viewed as an integral and useful forum for discussion among special interest groups, particularly between labor and management, and for gauging their opinion or gaining their acceptance on particular matters.

Composition. Members of the ESC should be nominated by their member nations and appointed by the Council of Ministers for a four-year renewable term. Members are to be divided into the three following groups. However, they are to act in their personal capacity, not under mandatory instruction, from these groups:

Employers—covering NAC industry, banking, financial institutions, and transport;

Workers—representing national trade union organizations, and;

Various Interests—comprising agriculture, artisans, small and medium industrial and commercial undertakings, and professional and consumer associations.

The ESC chair should rotate among representatives of the three aforementioned groups.

Responsibilities. ESC must be consulted by either the Council of Ministers or the Commission whenever desirable. The Commission and the Council should also be able to consult the ESC on any other matter they consider appropriate and the ESC should have the right to deliver (nonbinding) opinions on its own initiative.

The ESC, unlike the Parliament, should not be able to delay legislation by withholding its opinion. The Commission and the Council can impose a deadline on the ESC, after which they can proceed without the ESC's opinion.

Voting and Functioning. Opinions of the ESC will be delivered only by the ESC in plenary session following review by the appropriate sections and after majority acceptance by ESC members.

The major work of the ESC should be done in policy review sections, for example, agriculture, economic, trade, public health, etc.

The ESC's work should be organized by a president and Bureau, elected by the Committee from its own membership for a two-year run. The Bureau should instruct the relevant ESC sections to review specific proposals and to draw up opinions. The ESC should also be assisted by a Secretariat, which should be headed by a secretary-general.

Plenary sessions, open to the public, should be held nine times each year at which time draft reports submitted by the sections should be considered.

The Court of Justice

The Court of Justice will be the supreme court having jurisdiction in matters relating to NAC law. It is the highest and ultimate interpreter of all laws and signed treaties of the New American Community and the final arbiter in disputes concerning NAC law. Its function is to ensure that NAC law is observed and uniformly applied throughout the NAC. To this end, it should exercise judicial review of the acts of the NAC's institutions, rule on nations' compliance with their obligations, and respond to national courts' requests for preliminary rulings on the interpretation of NAC law.

Composition. The Court will have an odd number of judges, initially two from each of Mexico, Canada, and the United States and an additional judge appointed on a rotation from one of the larger nations. The judges will be appointed by mutual agreement of the NAC governments for a six-year renewable term. The president of the Court will be appointed by the judges from amongst themselves, for a three-year renewable term. The judges will be required to act impartially and independently of their national governments in the best interests of the New American Community.

The Court will also have six advocates-general, to assist the Court by giving reasoned opinions on cases brought before the Court prior to the Court's ruling.

The Court shall be divided into six distinct chambers which will make preparatory investigations and hear specific types of cases. The more important cases will be heard by the entire Court (in plenary session).

Jurisdiction: judicial review of the acts of NAC institutions. The Court should be able to annul any act of the Commission or the Council if it infringes NAC law. An action should also be brought if the Commission or the Council fail to act. Such actions can be brought by NAC institutions or nations. Individuals and firms (natural or legal persons) should also be able to bring this type of action, but only if they can prove that they are directly and individually concerned.

The Court should also hear cases against a NAC country for failure to comply with its obligations. Such cases can be brought by NAC institutions or nations, but not by individuals or companies. If the Court finds that a nation has not fulfilled its obligations, the NAC country must take the necessary measures to comply with the Court's final judgment.

Should a legal action in a national court produce a question regarding a possible conflict between NAC and national law, the national court may request a "preliminary ruling" from the Court of Justice on the correct interpretation under NAC law. This would be a preliminary ruling procedure, giving individual and firms indirect access to the Court of Justice, where the validity of a national statute or NAC measure can be tested, while they have very limited direct access to the Court.

The Court may impose fines for infringements, but national courts are entrusted with enforcing the judgments of the Court, which should have no enforcement authority of its own. A second (lower) court should be considered to both ease the caseload of the Court of Justice and to hear cases concerning disputes between NAC institutions, employers, and workers.

The Court should continuously pronounce its goals and principles. Primary should be that NAC law takes precedence over conflicting national laws (even if the latter are more recent or of a constitutional nature), and that NAC laws have direct effect, automatically conferring rights and obligations on individuals.

The Court of Auditors

Such a court should be independently responsible for examining the accounts, revenues, and expenditures of all NAC institutions and other

NAC bodies. It should publish its findings in an annual report. The Court of Auditors should have twelve members, appointed to six-year terms by the Council in consultation with the Parliament.

The New American Community Bank (NACB)

The New American Community Bank (NACB) should be an independent NAC institution of which the NAC nations are members. The NACB should raise money on the capital markets and grant loans and loan guarantees on a non-profit basis to facilitate the financing of projects in the NAC's less-developed regions; projects called for in the progressive establishment of a common market that cannot be financed by one NAC nation; projects in the interest of several NAC nations; and occasionally, development projects in non-member countries.

The NAC's Board of Governors should consist of the national finance ministers.

Appropriately, the above suggestions will have to be negotiated by the founding nations of the NAC. The "Why" questions must be answered, but the NAC structure is the answer to "How." "How" represents the mechanism, the means by which the successes and failures of the New American Community will ultimately be measured.

9

LEGAL INSTRUMENTS OF THE NEW AMERICAN COMMUNITY

REGULATIONS, DIRECTIVES, DECISIONS, OPINIONS AND RECOMMENDATIONS

The New American Community's body of laws shall consist of a Treaty establishing the NAC, legislation as adopted by its Council and the Commission, judgments of the Court of Justice, and conventions and international agreements entered into by the NAC. The Treaty should stipulate that, in order to carry out their task in accordance with the provisions of the Treaty, the Council and the Commission shall adopt legislation in the form of regulations, directives, decisions, opinions and recommendations.

In addition to the form of legislation, also important is the legal basis of the proposed measure. Depending on the content and aims, proposals for legislation should be based on one or another of the Articles found in the Treaty. These Articles in turn shall determine the legislative procedure that should be followed for adoption of any proposal as NAC law.

Regulations

Regulations shall be binding in their entirety, and should be directly applicable to all NAC nations, *i.e.*, they are automatically valid and have the force of law throughout the NAC without any further action necessary from national legislatures. They shall confer rights and impose obligations on NAC nations, national authorities, and individuals in the same manner as national legislation.

Directives

Directives should be used as means of action for achieving standardization of laws, and are to be the most common form of instrument used for measures to establish a unified market in the NAC.

Directives should be binding on NAC countries as to the objectives to be achieved, but the means to achieve them are left to NAC nations, which must implement them through national legislation. Member nations shall be required to notify the Commission about the national measures taken for their implementation.

Directives shall take effect upon notification to the NAC country to which they are addressed and usually specify a time period for implementation. It should be noted that should this create a right for individuals or firms, it can bring legal action against a government for not implementing, or incorrectly implementing, a NAC Directive by the stated deadline.

Decisions

Decisions shall be individual acts binding upon the entity to which they are addressed: nation, individual, or firm. They are to be often used in antitrust proceedings to declare an agreement void and to impose fines or penalties on corporations. They are also to be used to set out guidelines for NAC institutions for the future formulation of legislative proposals.

Opinions and Recommendations

Opinions and Recommendations shall *not* be binding. Opinions are to be the expression of a point of view, for example, how to promote co-operation in the NAC social field. Recommendations are a means of indirect action toward standardization of laws, for example, to prevent a NAC country from adopting a measure that will distort competition.

THE CREATION OF NEW AMERICAN COMMUNITY LAW

Introduction

The process for adopting legislation will be as follows. The Commission shall propose legislation and the Council of Ministers decide on it, after consulting the "advisory" bodies, the Parliament and the Economic and Social Committee.

All involved institutions, especially the Commission and the Council, should be in continuous dialogue, and that to follow a given measure, contact should be maintained with all institutions simultaneously.

The procedure for adopting a proposal for NAC legislation shall differ according to the type of measure and the article of the original Treaty on which the proposal is based.

Factors shall include:

1. Whether the Council or the Commission adopts the legislation. Although in some cases, the Commission may adopt legislation, in most cases adoption by the Council shall be required.
2. Adoption of measures shall be by a qualified majority.
3. Proposed measures shall be reviewed twice, by both the Parliament and the Council.

The Legislative Process

1. *The Commission drafts.* Drafts or working documents are to be produced in the appropriate Directorate-General (DG), in cooperation with other relevant DGs, and generally after consulting with other institutions and interested parties. They shall only become official proposals after being approved by the Commission itself (although agreement may be reached at the Cabinet level and require only formal approval by the Commissioners). Once approved, they are to be issued as Commission Documents and referred to the Council for consideration.

2. *The Council of Ministers shall refer the proposal to the Parliament for its first reading,* (in some cases to the Economic and Social Committee). The Council shall not act until it receives the opinion of the Parliament. As there shall be no time limit at this stage, the Parliament can delay legislation by delaying its opinion. By contrast, the Economic and Social Committee shall not be empowered to delay NAC legislation. The Council and the Commission shall be able to impose a deadline on the ESC, after which they can proceed without its opinion.

Having received the opinions of these advisory bodies, the Council shall assign the proposal to a working group of national representatives and experts and Commission representatives. The working group's conclusions shall be submitted to the Committee of Regular Officials (CORO), and if necessary, for debate in the Council. The Council shall then adopt a common position on the proposal, by qualified majority, although unanimity shall be required if the Council is amending the Commission's proposal.

3. This common position will then be referred back to the Parliament for a second reading. The Parliament will then have three months to approve, reject, or propose amendments to the common position.

If the Parliament approves the common position, or does not act, the Council will adopt the measure, according to its common position.

If the Parliament rejects the common position, the Council can only adopt it by unanimity.

If the Parliament amends the common position, the Commission must, within one month, reexamine its proposal, taking into account the Parliament's amendments. The Commission will then forward its reexamined proposal to the Council, along with the Parliament amendments which it shall not have incorporated into this revised proposal. The Council will now have three months to act. It will either:

—adopt this reexamined proposal (with no changes) by qualified majority;

—adopt it by unanimity if amending the reexamined proposal (including when the Council adopts Parliament amendments rejected by the Commission) or;

—fail to adopt the proposal, in which case it shall lapse.

This cooperation procedure, with its second reading, shall result in increased Parliamentary power—desirable matter as the Parliament shall represent the masses in the NAC. If the Parliament proposes amendments, 9and the Commission agrees with them, incorporating them into its revised proposal, the Council can only reject them by unanimity. Therefore, the Parliament will seek agreement with the Commission in advance on amendments. If the Commission refuses to support Parliament's amendments, Parliament can reject the common position, endangering the fate of the measure, which can only then be adopted if there is unanimous agreement in the Council. Directives will then be implemented by NAC nations through the adoption of national legislation.

This guidepost of legislative decisionmaking follows traditional methodology for incorporating changes into the founding Treaty. Rightfully so, founding members of the New American Community will spend endless hours picking at each of these entries, for they represent what the thinking of the day is willing to enter into debate. The regulations, directives, decisions, opinions and recommendations are the instruments that determine the future direction of the New American Community.

10

ELIMINATING BORDER BARRIERS AND FISCAL CONTROLS

To assure the smooth evolution of a common market in North America, and then onto other nations in the central and southern regions there must exist a provision for the free movement of goods, persons, services, and capital.

Presently, although accelerated by free-trade accords, customs posts and borders between the U.S., Mexico, and Canada continue to exist because they are a convenient point to exercise the fiscal, commercial, economic, health, police controls, and formalities which are thought to remain necessary. However, there is a substantial cost to industry alone of frontier-crossing requirements that may be as high as 5 percent of the volume of intra-North America trade.

The time is arriving when we must set the ambitious target of creating the necessary conditions for abolition of many of the present controls and formalities and of transferring others to points within the three countries where they can be performed with greater convenience and less cost to businesses. Later, when refined, these approaches will usher in similar abolitions throughout Central and South American nations.

BORDER BARRIERS

The physical barriers encountered at the borders between the three nations affect both goods and individuals. Border customs controls carry out a number of commercial functions: they make border collections of duties viable; they control the flow of farm items allowing different price levels for the same products to exist across member nations; they check plants and animals to preserve different health levels in different nations; they check trucks for road transport licenses; and they protect the trade regimes that individual nations may have with countries that are not participants in the Community.

However one analyzes the value of border crossings and the funds collected there, such customs posts are above all a matter of taxes. Since taxes are the primary civilian prerequisite of sovereignty, this issue has given nations their right to independence and justified their existence over and over again. Therefore, reducing and eventually eliminating customs throughout an internal market would put an end to much of this.

Borders do not divide markets, they separate different nations that they protect. The fear is that regulations can outline the responsibilities, but a watchdog may be needed to prevent governments from finding substitutes for them.

Goods

In the case of goods, checks and controls are carried out for a number of purposes: accounting for the incidence of value added taxes and duties on imports and exports, the gathering of trade statistics, the implementation of quantitative restrictions on imports, the administration of transport policy, to name but a few. The performance of these checks and controls requires commercial vehicle drivers to carry extensive documentation, especially when crossing from Mexico into the United States, and to wait their turn in long lines in front of customs posts. The resulting familiar lines of trucks at the frontiers represent costs to the economy in terms of goods, vehicles, and drivers which are immobilized. Many of the controls and checks can be transferred to other locations away from the physical frontiers; this alleviates but does not erase the problem of border-related controls. What is needed is to coordinate policy and bring national legislation closer together so as to eliminate the barriers and controls in connection with crossing borders.

As with the European Community, Mexico, Canada, and the United States should have, at least in the early stages of the NAC, a Single Administrative Document which is to be used for all consignments of goods crossing internal borders. This will provide a considerable saving in paperwork, time, and effort.

Regulations are ultimately needed in the control of goods:

—development of a single administrative document

—abolishing the requirement for a guarantee of payment of duties and fiscal charges arising from internal transit operations within the three nations

—ultimately abolishing exit customs formalities and reducing the number of checks at borders

—significantly reducing customs formalities at internal land borders by requiring only a single customs check (instead of one on both exit and entry), and enabling officials of one of the three nations to act in the place of officials of an adjoining nation with no legal effect loss

—abolition of controls relating to means of transport, and

—the standardization or abolition of all remaining import formalities and controls on goods between the United States, Mexico, and/or Canada.

Still to be resolved will be a clearer definition of free trade. For example, does it mean that U.S. firms have a right to sell anything in Canada that conforms to Canadian rules, or does it mean that U.S. firms can sell in Canada whatever they choose to sell in the States? It allows governments to block imports on grounds of public policy and, on the other hand, it says such bans must not amount to arbitrary discrimination or disguised restrictions on trade.

Individuals

The New American Community must make it easier for people to travel around the NAC. The solution requires considerable political undertaking. The questions of crime and of illegal immigration control remain important to all nations. Does a common policy on immigration demand a common policy on visas for citizens from a given nation outside the NAC? And does a common visa policy imply a common foreign policy toward that nation? Would policing of borderless NAC nations require cross-border operations by police forces of the entire NAC? And does that require a standardization of national criminal law and its enforcement? These critical questions persist.

The New American Community without frontiers has both advantages and risks. One advantage is that it forces NAC participating nations to take a hard look at the jurisdictional differences that divide them, and demands an answer to how important they really are. Few differences get left unexplored, and, to the extent that they are either standardized away or left at the mercy of open frontiers, the idea of an open NAC is advanced. A major risk is that national differences won't fade away, and that the quest for the frontier-free idea leads to more expensive, bureaucratic and generally inconvenient ways of enforcing them than the borders were in the first place.

In the case of people, the passport controls, again, especially between the U.S. and Mexico, and Mexico and Canada, the search of baggage and vehicles, the customs checks on purchases are a permanent reminder that the northern hemisphere is divided into sovereign nations. In a true New

American Community, the ever closer union, such frontier formalities have no place. Citizens from all three nations should not have to produce documents of identity and nationality and obtain customs clearance of goods in their baggage when passing from one country to another. Of course, certain national protective measures, for example, those controlling terrorism, drugs smuggling, and other forms of crime, will continue to be necessary in a unified market. It is convenience which dictates that these measures function at borders, and that they can be applied elsewhere so as to eliminate border police checks.

Procedurally, it is recommended that removing border controls of people occur in two stages: border formalities will be made more flexible and less systematic and, when external borders and cooperation between the three national authorities reach appropriate levels, the border controls can be totally abolished.

Regulations are ultimately needed in the control of people of these three countries, in the following areas:

—abolishing controls on the possession of weapons at intra-North American borders. (This should not affect the right of an individual country to take other measures to prevent illegal trade in weapons.)
—making travel and tourism within the three nations easier by increasing tax-free allowances.
—increasing the amount of tax relief from excise duties, etc., available on small consignments of a non-commercial character sent from one private person to another across internal borders. This will keep the real value constant, taking cost of living increases into account.
—amending exemptions in favor of imports so as to be consistent with certain customs exemptions and to introduce specific intra-North American exemptions.
—standardizing and relaxing certain formalities needed to obtain tax exemptions on permanent imports into another country of the personal property of an individual.
—extending existing tax exemption for private vehicles that are temporarily imported into another NAC country.
—easing controls and formalities for nationals of the three countries by abolishing all police and customs formalities.

Other regulations will be needed dealing with drugs, status of third country nationals, right of asylum and the status of refugees, national visa policies, and rules concerning extradition.

BORDER FISCAL CONTROLS

Fiscal controls are among the most important functions performed at or related to borders. As long as indirect taxes on goods, and excise duties in particular differ significantly between the three countries of North America, there will be an incentive for purchasers to buy goods in lower tax nations. This leads to distortions in trade patterns which make no sense in a unified market and also creates revenue problems for all three countries. These problems are presently solved by means of their fiscal borders. If the indirect tax levels of the different countries are sufficiently close together, purchasing decisions will no longer be distorted by the tax component of prices. In that situation, the tax aspects of intra-North America imports and exports will not need to be handled at internal borders.

Making these decisions easier, we must be comforted to know that the European system of value-added tax does not truly exist in North America and therefore need not restrain constructive movement in dealing with exports and imports.

We must find a mechanism to standardize the structure of the principal excise duties. Then, as a second step, a standardization of the rates of excise duties will be required. This would necessitate the linkage of the bonded warehouse system which is currently used for controlling movement of excise goods. Once measures on excise duties are in place, one of the major obstacles to the elimination of border controls will have disappeared.

Regulations will be needed:

—to introduce a standardized structure for excise duties on alcohol in order to eliminate distortions in conditions of competition

—to bring the three nations' taxes on alcoholic drinks together with a view to eliminating distortions of competition

—to facilitate future standardization of excise duties, with a view to eliminating distortions of competition

—to proceed to a stage in standardizing the structure of the three nations' systems of excise duties on cigarettes

—to introduce common rates of excise duty on alcohol for the purpose of establishing an internal market without frontiers

—to standardize the rates of the excise duties applied to cigarettes by the three participating nations

—to standardize the structure of excise duties on cigars, cigarillos, smoking tobacco, chewing tobacco, and snuff and bring the excise duties closer together

—to standardize the structure of excise duties on mineral oils (leaded gasoline, unleaded gasoline, diesel, heavy fuel oil, heating gas oil, liquid gas used as road fuel, methane used as road fuel, kerosene when used as a propellant and for other purposes) as a preparation for standardization of rates; the final objective being to eliminate distortions of conditions of competition

—to introduce common rates of excise duties on mineral duties

—to create a committee to enable the New American Community to adopt a simple and accelerated procedure with technical measures required for the implementation of directives on excise duties.

The initial steps to lowering barriers must begin within the internal market of NAC participating nations. Once accomplished, or in tandem with the external aspects of a free market, a realistic and profitable scheme will emerge. At first, disparities between nations in their economic well-being will strain all attempts to eliminate such border and fiscal barriers, but sensible and determined approaches to balance out these differences can be created, with both short- and long-term strategies to smooth out inequities.

11

THE PASSAGE TO EDUCATION

A critical message has often been sent to bring the "have-nots" into the 21st century. Central to this challenge, and a counter force of rebellion is to upgrade each person's educational opportunity to parallel his or her aptitude and personal drives for success. The disparity throughout the Americas is appalling. Each nation has its shame to live with, which has smothered millions and dismissed them from the ladder of a raised standard of living.

With the first phase of the New American Community purporting to unite the trade and economies of Canada, Mexico, and the United States, the interdependence must also be reflected in an educational cooperation plan to make a free-trade zone prosper.

SOUTH OF THE BORDER

Where will the future leaders in industry and government come from to run these massive organizations? It is unconscienable to think that the better educated in one of the three nations will dominate the businesses in either of the other two countries. Imperialism, more specifically knowledge imperialism, will not be tolerated, nor in the long run will it prove productive. An educated workforce able to face a multinational environment should be at the forefront of our strategy.

Within Mexico, as is found throughout Latin American nations, there is a growing demand on the part of students and adults for greater exchanges with U.S. colleges and universities. The days of resistance because of Marxist leanings being found in U.S. higher education institutions that brainwashed cultural and economic imperialism are dwindling. The trend clearly points to an ever increasing desire to study in the States.

Part of this phenomenon is an outgrowth of the newer leadership in Mexico (and also throughout the Americas) that have received a significant share of their higher education across their border. The list of government leaders having received graduate training in the U.S. includes the President, who went to Harvard University, the Chief of Cabinet (Stanford University), the Minister of the Treasury (Massachusetts Institute of Technology), the Minister of Education (Tulane University), the Minister of Budget (Yale University), and the Mayor of Mexico City (Princeton University). Today, Mexican leaders are urging the greatest cooperative programs in education with the States and Canada that have ever been noted. They want formal arrangements to exchange faculty and scholars-in-residence for collaborative research and for library development.

Another motive is to encourage the better understanding of Mexico's people, culture, and history, by an increased flow of U.S. students and faculty to its universities. According to Alan Adelman, director of the Institute of International Education's Office for Mexico and Central America, "only 5 percent of all U.S. students in study-abroad programs now attend Mexican institutions, despite their comparatively low cost and the fact that Spanish is the second language of the United States . . . "

In the 1960s and 1970s the ratio of Asian students to Latin American students in U.S. colleges and universities was approximately two to one. The economic crises of the 1980s and the increasing costs of tuition and room and board in U.S. schools combined to make it very difficult for any middle-class or poorer family to send their child to the States for higher education. In the mid- and late 1980s, Asian student enrollment in the U.S. rose to almost 50 percent of the total of all foreign students studying here. The overall enrollment of Latin American students continued to fall. In 1990 the ratio of Asian and Latin American students studying in the United States was six to one. Considering only graduate education the case appears to be far worse and therefore more serious, with a ratio of nine Asian students to every one from Latin America. The ratio of Chinese graduate students to Mexican graduate students ran 13 to 1 in 1990.

CROSS-BORDER EDUCATION

An all-out stampede must proceed to overcome the shortcomings and disgrace in these figures. We all must strive to encourage more exchanges at both the undergraduate and graduate levels from both Mexico and Canada and to encourage more U.S. and Canadian professors, researchers, and students to cross into Mexico for further higher-education studies.

Experiments and past experience in these areas have been a dismal failure. Borrowing on the creative thinking of others, particularly in the European Community, who have spent decades finding a partial solution to this dilemma, the leadership in the New American Community should draw from what is determined beneficial and push aside those efforts of others that are either inappropriate or prove unworthy of continuing efforts.

TO EMULATE IS TO FLATTER

In 1976, the European Community passed a resolution identifying the first program of educational cooperation, including educating migrant workers and their families: forming closer relations between various educational systems, especially higher education; improving the teaching of foreign languages; encouraging the mobility of students; the mutual recognition of diplomas and periods of study in Community nations; and providing equal opportunity for all to all forms of education. It is time that the United States, Canada, and Mexico, and eventually all Latin American nations, declare a parallel position. In time, the level of success will be measured by the competence of the educated.

Another effort of the European Community to study closely is COMETT. The Community Program in Education and Training for Technology (COMETT) was approved in July 1986 to encourage cooperation between universities and industry at the European level; to promote a European identity through student placement in firms located in other member states; to encourage economies of scale through the joint organization of new training programs, improving the initial training of students and the continued training of skilled personnel and executive staff; to develop the level of training in response to technological and social changes; to strengthen and diversify possibilities for training at local, regional, and national levels; and to exploit the opportunities offered by new information and communication technologies. A minimum of $258 million had been allocated by the European Community through 1994. This is certainly a program worthy of consideration for the NAC.

The NAC should evolve a required program of cross-border schooling. This might parallel the E.C.'s ERASMUS. Headquartered in Belgium, the European Action Scheme for the Mobility of University Students (ERASMUS) was adopted on June 15, 1987 and involves 3,600 higher education establishments and some 6 million students, primarily to encourage students to do part of their studies in a university in another member state. This is the model that should be studied most carefully to witness the system of transferable academic credits and the recognition of college diplomas.

Designed to enable university students to spend a year of their university studies in another one of the ll member states of the E.C., as a first step in the free exchange of scholarly credentials, the ERASMUS program in 1987 sent 16,000 students from both universities and technical colleges to schools in other member countries for up to six months. To qualify for an ERASMUS grant, which ranges from approximately $280 to $700 a year, students must enroll in one of the more than 1,000 ERASMUS-approved university programs. The grants are designed to cover travel expenses and any differences in the cost of attending school abroad instead of at home. None of the participating universities charge tuition fees. Of 32,000 applicants in 1989, ERASMUS financed 28,000 students and teachers. During the 1989 academic year, 4,046 university teachers visited a university in another E.C. state. In addition, the E.C. Commission granted about $600,000 to European university and student associations enabling over 20,000 young Europeans to study in another Community state during the 1989–1990 academic year. The goal is to sponsor 160,000 people by 1992.

These comparisons are but a few that should be made. Other nations provide unique efforts demonstrating that cross-border education can succeed. We in the New American Community have suffered from a resistance to accept that other countries have an educational product worthy of our attention. This must change.

MEETING THE CHALLENGE

Cooperation between the U.S. and Mexico moves along at an ever increasing speed. Enrollment of Mexican students at Texas colleges, for example, and universities near the common border has increased considerably since 1985. A Texas law was passed allowing Mexicans who were able to demonstrate financial hardship only to pay Texas resident tuition fees. At the University of Texas at El Paso alone, about 700 Mexican students are enrolled, 11 percent of all Mexican nationals attending colleges in the U.S.

Community colleges in the States that are located within easy access to the 2,000 mile border with Mexico assist in the training of Mexican workers, primarily employed in the so-called "screwdriver plants" (the maquiladoras) in computers, drafting, electronics, robotics, plastics-molding technology, accounting, and international trade and transportation.

A landmark agreement was signed in January 1990 by the Institute for International Education, the United States Information Agency, and the Mexican Council of Science and Technology that will permit up to 250 Mexican doctoral students to study at U.S. universities over the coming eight years. Preference for study will be in science and technology areas. Then, in November 1990 President Bush and President Salinas signed an agreement establishing a Fulbright Commission in Mexico, designed to increase considerably the exchange of Fulbright recipients between the two nations.

Working together, we must develop a degree program in which students from Mexico, Canada, and the United States could complete part of their studies in the other two nations. Alan Adelman has a substitute word for the E.C.'s ERASMUS program. He would call it the Continental Organization of Leading Universities for the Mobility of Bilingual University Scholars, or COLUMBUS for short, a worthy NAC effort.

In the 21st century we must have our own continental academic common market. If the E.C. can do it with 12 nations, 9 official languages, myriad cultural differences and traditions, certainly we in the New American Community can exploit the potential for more academic integration of a less linguistically and culturally diverse three nations. Once accomplished, other countries within the hemisphere will enter the growing mix of university students and faculty. From three languages, the shift will move to four; from three nations a cross-cultured educated population will be found in thirty-three countries.

12

INDUSTRIAL COOPERATION

Although some progress has already been made in cooperation between businesses with fair-trade agreements between the three nations of founding members of the New American Community, much more remains to be done. Continued upgrading of these relationships still exists, caused by excessive legal, fiscal and administrative problems, and conflicting attitudes and habits.

Forming a NAC will properly require firms becoming more and more involved in all matters of intra-North American operations. There will be an ever increasing number of links with associated enterprises, creditors and parties in each of the three nations, to be followed by others. Can anyone tell a sovereign government how to spend its own money, on its own firms, on its own soil? Yes. In such a scenario, the NAC executives would tell firms to scale back their cash they give to firms, even to recover subsidies from company treasuries. The NAC also will have the power to veto and block all mergers with a combined worth exceeding an established amount.

The shock passes, the reasons are sound. If you remove national trade barriers but permit the capacity of governments to interfere with trade by supporting unfairly one industry against another, or allow firms to carve up markets and fix distribution you have the same effect of destroying a common market that could be unified. The NAC must ban any aid granted by a member nation or through resources in any form whatsoever which distorts or threatens to distort competition by favoring certain undertakings or the production of certain goods. This applies to both the public and private sectors within the NAC.

What is needed is an environment that favors the development of cooperation between individual firms crossing borders. Such an ambiance is necessary for several reasons. The elimination of internal borders, the movement of goods and capital, freedom of establishment, and the freedom to supply services are fundamental to the creation of the internal market and will confer enormous benefits on suppliers and consumers of goods and services. It will also create opportunities and incentives for cooperation between businesses in the three nations, for example, where complementary expertise and resources are identified. This cooperation could take a variety of forms ranging from mergers or the incorporation of joint subsidiaries to ad hoc cooperation on specific projects. The benefits of such cooperation would not only be felt within the New American Community, in its northern, central, and southern nations, it would also strengthen the position of the Americas' businesses when competing on world markets.

The elimination of internal frontiers is not sufficient to create the optimum environment for cross-border cooperation between companies. At present there are few truly appropriate forms for such cooperation. Company mergers across borders involve the application of differing national laws and often have tax implications which can act as a severe disincentive. The setting up of a joint subsidiary involves at least one partner in an unfamiliar legal system while, again, the tax implications may act as a disincentive. When businesses wish to pursue jointly a single activity there is no appropriate and administratively straightforward corporate form for doing so. Numerous potential joint projects have failed to get off the ground because of such problems.

The existence of differences in patent, trademark, and copyright laws also has a direct, negative effect on intra-North American trade and on the ability of businesses to treat each other's nations' firms as a single and unified market. Multiple applications for patents and trademarks, and the correspondingly multiplied fees, create an administrative and financial burden which also psychologically perpetuates the traditional perception of separate national markets. In the intellectual property field, advances in technology, particularly in the areas of computer software, microcircuits, and biotechnology, create the risk that separate intellectual property systems will adapt in different ways. This would generate uncertainty about the level of protection of innovation, uncertainty which would act as a disincentive to both the investment and cooperation between businesses in each of the three NAC nations. Regulations are needed in the fields of company law, taxation, and intellectual property to prepare for a more equitable and smooth flowing path of industrial cooperation.

COMPANY LAW

A void presently exists within the NAC for cross-border operations and cooperation between firms in these different countries, resulting in multinational projects being unable to get off the ground. In order to satisfy the needs of a genuine market within these three, and later other member nations, companies must be able to cooperate, set up subsidiaries, merge, and generally restructure across internal borders without unnecessary formalities of a purely technical nature.

Needs in company law include:

—to create a new legal entity to facilitate and encourage cross-border cooperation. This will benefit businesses which do not wish to merge or form joint subsidiaries, but wish to carry out certain activities in common

—to create a New American Community Company with its own legislative framework. This will permit firms incorporating in any hemisphere nation to merge and form a holding company or a joint subsidiary without suffering from conflicting national laws

—to ensure that managers of public limited liability firms are effectively supervised on behalf of the shareholders and to ensure employee participation in the management of such firms

—presently, it is difficult and discouraging for firms in the three NAC nations to merge. A regulation is needed to standardize the laws on cross-border mergers of public limited companies so as to facilitate this process. To protect shareholders, creditors, and employees when all the assets and liabilities in a firm are transferred to another firm in a different nation

—to relieve foreign branches of firms of the obligation to publish branch accounts, so as to facilitate the freedom of establishment

—to extend national legislation relating to annual company accounts and consolidated accounts to partnerships. This will ensure that certain types of partnerships, all of whose unlimited members are constituted as limited liability companies, do not avoid corporate disclosure

—to structure a procedure for firms to compete that are wholly owned subsidiaries of centrally managed multinational companies in other nations

—to establish a method of equity in the liquidation of firms, takeover bids, and procedures for changing company laws.

Laws must be put in place dealing with:

—direct effect—to establish the right of individuals and firms to invoke NAC law in national courts, thereby allowing citizens to do their own policing

—primacy effect—to establish that NAC law overrides the national laws of member nations.

INTELLECTUAL PROPERTY

The existing differences between the three NAC nations' intellectual property laws have an adverse impact on intra-NAC trade and on the ability of firms to treat a unified market as a single environment for their activities. In the field of trademarks, the existence of differing national systems creates obstacles to NAC-wide marketing, in addition to cumbersome and costly administrative and legal burdens. A unified NAC market requires a single trademark system for firms trading throughout the NAC. It also requires more uniformity in national trademark systems for firms who, although not trading throughout the NAC, do have commercial activities in at least another country of the NAC.

The confusion in dealing with intellectual property is further complicated by the need to provide protection to inventions in new technologies such as computer software, microcircuits, and biotechnology. These technologies were not in existence when the present intellectual property laws were originally drafted, and so methods for legal protection are obscure. Needs of intellectual property include:

—to create a trademark applicable throughout the NAC. This will remove the current requirement to make separate applications for trademarks in each country

—to ensure that registered trademarks enjoy the same protection under the legal systems of all the countries of the NAC

—to specify the fees payable to a NAC trademark office and the methods of payment

—to standardize national legislation regarding the protection of the topographies (design) of semiconductor products and to provide protection for the creator of the design, thereby allowing for the free movement of semiconductors within the NAC

—to standardize national legislation regarding the innovations within the biotechnology field

—to standardize national legislation regarding the innovations within the computer field.

TAXATION

In a unified market, business decisions should be taken on commercial grounds which have uniform tax considerations throughout the NAC. The current differences in company tax between NAC nations can distort investment decisions and conditions of competition. There is a widespread feeling throughout the Americas that the fiscal environment discourages risk capital and innovation. This compares badly with that of the NAC's major competitors.

A critical problem in cross-border operations is the risk of double taxation, due to differences in national tax laws. Much work is still required in this area. Needs in taxation include:

—to create a system whereby the profits of a subsidiary firm in one country within NAC distributed to the parent company in another NAC nation are exempt from withholding tax on dividends and corporation tax in the hands of the parent company

—to eliminate the source of double taxation within NAC. Some multinational firms currently suffer from double taxation because national tax authorities adjust transfer prices between subsidiaries in the group

—to resolve the tax problems resulting from NAC nations' tax treatment of cross-border restructuring of firms

—to standardize and liberalize NAC nations' laws governing the carry-over of losses. This is of special importance because of its effect on the investment capability and competitiveness of businesses

—to standardize indirect taxation on transactions in securities. Movements of capital will no longer be distorted by differing national taxes which currently result in double taxation and discrimination

—to develop a system dealing with enterprise taxation

—to standardize the tax base of enterprises.

PUBLIC PROCUREMENT

It is estimated that the total value of government procurement including contracts awarded by firms in the public sector of Mexico, Canada, and the United States could run as high as 15 percent of NAC's gross domestic product, as is the case in the European Community. Also, as found in the E.C., under five percent of public procurement contracts are awarded to firms from a member state other than the member state advertising the tender. The same, unless resisted, will occur within the New American Community.

This lack of open and effective competition is one of the most obvious and anachronistic obstacles to the completion of a NAC unified market. As well as increasing costs for the procuring bodies, the lack of intra-NAC competition in certain key industries like telecommunications discourages the emergence of NAC firms which are competitive on world markets. Any procurement program should require:

—a broadening of the scope of the obligations that already supposedly exist and block any loopholes in them

—equipping itself with greater powers to enforce those obligations

—improving the redress that disappointed or disenfranchised bidders will have if they feel themselves unfairly excluded

—extending open procurement to businesses that have remained exempt from it until now.

Needs in public procurement include:

—to increase openness of procedures and practices in awarding public supply contracts. To develop the conditions of effective competition in the public procurement markets, define and reduce the extent of industry sectors which are currently exempt, and to specify a time-limit for introducing further provisions for these sectors. To make use of the open procedure rule (as contrasted with restricted procedure or negotiated procedure) and to create a negotiating procedure in order to limit the use of the single tender procedure

—to ensure that decisions for procurement of public works are taken on the best commercial grounds and do not create a bureaucratic burden. Consequently, to increase the openness of award procedures and improve information, offering better opportunities for participation of interested firms and establishing a better base for pursuing infringement

—to increase substantially the guarantees of openness and non-discrimination in public procurement. To ensure that any offenses committed during the tender award procedures are effectively and rapidly censured

—to strengthen and improve existing provisions by limiting the exclusions, reducing the thresholds, and introducing new procedures

—to ensure that there are effective remedies if there is national or other discrimination in awarding contracts

—to remove the concept of excluded sectors

—to extend the scope as it applies to transportation, energy, water, and telecommunications.

To a large extent, the success of a New American Community will be determined by the inroads and successes within the sphere of industrial cooperation. Clear evidence of an upward shift in this collaboration is critical for mass support. Any weakening of industrial cooperative procedures will undermine future programs requiring faith, trust, and shared energies. The less sophisticated Central and South American nations will be watching closely to see how the northern hemisphere countries adjust to required shifts in behavior and industrial policy. Once procedures are firmly established and proven appropriate, other nations will follow with conviction and high hopes.

13

A HEALTHIER COMMUNITY

The maintenance of border controls on animals and plant products perpetuates the costs and disadvantages of separate national markets and increases the risk of disease and contamination to the general public. Substantial further action is needed. A New American Community common market for trade in live animals and animal and plant products cannot be said to exist if there are hold-ups, administrative burdens, and substantial costs each time goods cross NAC borders.

THE PROBLEM

Nothing in commerce and trade is more emotional to its citizens than the idea of a hazard to their health being imported from another country. Nothing is more likely to make NAC governments resist the lifting of their national border controls on animal and plant diseases as well as many other hazards than the feeling that they cannot trust each other to tell the truth.

In the veterinary and plant sector the objective should be to create an environment in which there is no difference between trade internally within the NAC and within any one country of the NAC. Veterinary and plant controls affect a wide range of activities in the farming, production, and processing of live animals and animal and plant products. Five areas require consideration: animal health, public health, animal welfare, zootechnics (pedigree and herd books), and plant health.

Presently at borders separating Mexico, Canada, and the United States, checks are made on imported veterinary and plant products. These often involve inspection of imports at frontiers or prohibition on food products which have not been produced in line with national requirements. With the NAC, these controls will have to be phased out in order to allow the free movement of goods and ensure that national health standards are not used as a non-tariff barrier. The aim, therefore, is to have one inspection and certification at the point of origin which is then accepted throughout the NAC. Eventually, when other Latin American nations are brought into the New American Community, similar and appropriate procedures will have to be put in place.

Not all is going well. The U.S. Government Accountability Project staff attorney and public education coordinator found that our food safety standards have been compromised since the U.S.-Canada Trade Accord took place in January 1989. According to Elaine Dodge and Christy Law, that same month the U.S. Agriculture Department's Food Safety and Inspection Service introduced "streamlined" procedures for inspecting meats at 17 Canadian border stations staffed with about a dozen inspectors. A twenty-five year inspector veteran from Montana refused entry to 1.9 million pounds of meat from Canada in 1989 and 2.5 million pounds in 1990, finding it unfit for consumption. Through April 1991, the inspector has rejected 684,000 pounds, most filled with pus-abscesses, sticky layers of bacteria leaving a stench, fecal contamination stains, blood, bruises, and metal shavings. Prior to the signing of the U.S.-Canadian trade accord, the U.S. Agriculture Department stopped every truck carrying meat at the border and selected samples for inspection. Since January 1989, inspectors usually check only one of every fifteen trucks crossing into the United States. In June 1990, 20,000 pounds of beef frankfurters from Ontario crossed into the States. Detection of the presence of listeria, a potentially deadly bacteria, and other dangerous poisons were discovered only after some of the food had been consumed.

Americans will not and should not tolerate such ineptness. Nothing can destroy the evolution of the New American Community quicker than a panic resulting from unhealthy food imports. Clearly, new guidelines will be needed to standardize NAC controls on the production, farming, and processing of food products deriving from animals and crops. This includes standardizing:

—methods for control of various diseases

—NAC approval of permitted treatments in farming, for example the controls on the use of hormones or pesticides

—animal pedigree and seed certification procedures

—health requirements in the processing and marketing of food originating from either animals or crops.

This approach will standardize essential requirements throughout the NAC in the production and processing of animal and plant products. At that time, member nations of the NAC will then be able to ensure animal health, public health, breeding and animal welfare by an appropriate method of confirming that the NAC requirements have been followed. This will permit the existing physical frontier controls on animal and plant products to be eliminated and replaced by the appropriate inspection at the point of origin, thus promoting free trade while maintaining health standards throughout the New American Community.

ANIMAL HEALTH CONTROLS

No symbol of a nation's fear of foreign contamination is more graphic than the snarling poster of a rabid dog that greets anyone who lands at an airport. To begin with, the NAC must develop a large body of legislation that is accepted by all involved member nations, providing health controls for agricultural animals, ensuring that food of animal origin is safe for consumers, concerning the breeding of animals and affected animal welfare. The various essential checks on compliance with this legislation have remained for the most part national. This has meant that when animals and animal products are traded across borders national authorities have carried out the veterinary checks and controls at frontier customs posts. This has created administrative burdens, costs, and delays which have no place in a unified market.

In the field of veterinary controls, further standardization of national laws and regulations is essential on veterinary requirements. This standardization must reach the point where it is possible for animals and animal products destined for export across NAC internal borders to be controlled and certified at the point of departure and require no further inspection. This certification would then be accepted throughout the NAC. Intra-NAC trade across borders of animals and animal products would thus become equivalent to national trade in these products. Imports from other non-NAC nations would upon arrival at a NAC border be checked to ensure compliance with NAC regulations. Once certified, these products would then be able to move within the NAC in the same way as any other NAC item.

Regulations on animal health controls needed include:

—measures designed to eradicate classical swine fever
—measures to deal with the outbreak of animal diseases to take into account classical swine fever(s)

—to develop a new type of heat treatment to those currently acceptable for preventing swine fever in meat products

—to develop measures to restrict the outbreak and spread of foot-and-mouth disease

—measures to effectively deal with Aujesky's disease affecting pig herds

—to complete the eradication of brucellosis, tuberculosis, and leucosis in cattle throughout the NAC

—to reduce the risk of spreading animal disease by standardizing NAC nations' rules for intra-NAC trade in semen; and standardizing rules for imports of semen from non-NAC nations

—to improve the required hygienic conditions under which fresh meat and poultry meat are produced in slaughterhouses and meat and poultry meat cutting plants, by requiring proprietors to conduct microbiological analysis as a means of achieving an objective analysis of the standard of hygiene

—to adopt a general uniform approach to detecting and limiting residues in meat and meat products in all NAC countries

—to protect the public from any dangers arising from the use of medicated feedingstuffs for animals intended for food production. Thus, to help ensure free competition in the keeping and rearing of farm animals

—to restrict the use of hormones for the fattening of livestock. These will be restricted to certain substances used to treat infertility under strictly controlled circumstances

—to eliminate national differences in health requirements concerning heat-treated milk (pasteurized, UHT, or sterilized) intended for internal NAC trade

—to standardize the health requirements to be met by egg products in the NAC

—to improve hygiene in establishments where fresh meat, poultry meat, and meat products are handled

—to permit NAC countries to authorize suitably qualified officials to be responsible for the supervision of meat products and poultry meat products inspection

—to update regulations to take into account new scientific and technological developments; to include certain meat-based preparations and precooked dishes not currently covered

—to standardize health requirements concerning frozen meat, standardize rules for possible additional requirements for ante mortem and post mortem inspection

—to introduce additional public health and animal health conditions for imports of meat items from outside NAC in order to avoid the introduction of certain diseases in Mexico, Canada, and the United States

—to standardize requirements for producing and marketing minced meat

—to facilitate the import of glands and other organs, including blood, for the pharmaceutical processing industry

—to standardize health requirements so as to prevent the consumption of fish and fish products contaminated by nematodes

—to undertake the same inspections of fresh meat intended for trade within Mexico, Canada, and the United States as are already required for fresh meat intended for intra-NAC trade. This should help to achieve free movement with the NAC

—to introduce further standardization in the pedigree requirement of cattle and their semen for breeding purposes

—to standardize requirements for breeding pigs so as to facilitate intra-NAC trade in these animals

—to standardize requirements for breeding sheep and goats so as to facilitate intra-NAC trade in these animals

—to standardize requirements for the transport of animals

—to standardize requirements for embryos of farm animals

—to standardize requirements for trade in shellfish

—to standardize requirements for labelling rules for food

—to standardize requirements for game and game meat

—to standardize requirements for trade in horses

—to standardize requirements for live poultry, poultry meat, and eggs

—to standardize requirements for trade in dogs and cats

—to extend NAC rules to national markets.

PLANT HEALTH CONTROLS

The only way of reconciling the differences in people's ideas of a given food is to describe it more carefully and let the consumer choose, rather than controlling ingredients. For example, Italy initially tried to block imports of pasta simply because it was made of soft wheat rather than the classic Italian ingredient of durum wheat. Ultimately, the resolution was based on the type of wheat being clearly listed on the pasta package, not that it was a non-traditional ingredient.

A classic battle is presently underway as the European Community integration rushes toward the end of 1992 and its 12 nation integration. In the normally placid countryside in northwestern France, where Camembert cheese is made, the bureaucrats from Brussels are antagonizing the farmers over bacteria counts and their use of tepid, raw milk. The E.C. seeks ways to protect all consumers in a unified Europe, or as the producers of 50 million boxes of camembert claim, it is an illustration of what is wrong with an emerging super-state that attempts to impose tedious uniformity. One must be sensitive to this latter position which appears to be a tug between northern Europe and its strict standards of hygiene, versus the more relaxed and flavor-rich south. The parallel might also be used with the New American Community. How the issue is resolved should become a case study for those planning future integrated cross-border systems.

If food moves more freely under policies of the New American Community, so too may hazards to the health of those who eat it spread unless protected. Presently Mexico, Canada, and the United States, in varying degrees, have a large body of legislation that provides health controls for crops and ensures that food derived from these plants is safe for consumers. However, the various essential controls on compliance with this legislation have remained national. This has meant that, when plants and products are traded across borders, which has usually been very limited, national authorities have carried out the plant health checks and controls at border customs posts. This has created administrative burdens, costs, and delays which have no place in a unified market.

In the field of plant health controls, further standardization of national laws and regulations on essential plant health requirements will be needed. This standardization must reach the point where it is possible for plants and plant products, destined for export across the NAC's internal borders, to be controlled and certified at the point of departure. The resulting certification then needs only to be checked at the point of import into the other two nations of the northern hemisphere. Within practical limits, a similar system should apply to imports from non-NAC nations.

It is critical therefore that the means be found to standardize NAC plant health inspectorate, and to evolve measures against the introduction of organisms harmful to plants or plant products:

—to prohibit the use of certain products in plant protection

—to lay down the maximum permissible levels of pesticide residues in and on fruit and vegetables

—to standarize provisions with NAC nations so as to achieve the free circulation of plant protection products in the NAC

—to improve the labelling of certified seeds

—to develop protective measures against the introduction of organisms that are harmful to plants

—to define common guidelines on acceptable additives in animal feedingstuffs

—to establish and monitor maximum levels for certain pesticide residues in cereal products

—to standardize the maximum levels of pesticides which are permitted in animal feedingstuffs

—to improve the uncovering of pesticide residues on fruits and vegetables

—to certify seedlings and reproductive materials of fruit plants and decorative plants

—to develop plant health certificates

—to deal with liability in respect of plant health

—to align standards of plant health

—to create a law on plant breeders rights.

Once integration commences, setting standards and procedures for guaranteeing the proper safeguards against animal and plant hazards, differences will immediately surface. It is critical that openness and precaution be the force behind all deliberations. Safe items in one nation can prove to be detrimental to a new population unexposed to problematic diseases. Once the irritant of growing controls is appreciated as a protector, nations of the NAC will become more tolerant of such activities, knowing that free trade of animal and plant products will become a welcomed event.

14

A COMMON MARKET FOR SERVICES

SETTING THE STAGE—AN ANALYSIS OF THE ISSUES

A unified market in the New American Community necessitates the free movement of goods, persons, services, and capital. The continued maintenance of barriers perpetuates the costs and disadvantages of separate national markets for services. There is a need for substantial action, for being free to establish a branch in another nation has little meaning if local regulations there prevent the branch from operating on an equal footing with local competitors.

The suggestions outlined below for financial, telecommunications, and transport services, and for the free movement of labor, are intended to increase competition, efficiency, and the choices available to people and business users in a unified NAC market. The range of services is essential in the economic and industrial development of the NAC. The goals sought with the completion of a unified market are not only to ensure development in this sector (in itself a creator of employment) but, most of all to guarantee the accessibility of services to industry which are cheaper, more efficient, and better suited to its needs.

Financial Liberties

Three financial liberties are called for in the NAC—freedom to establish branches abroad, freedom to sell across borders, and freedom to move money. Financial services do form an important element in the economy of all NAC nations as a source of employment and of net exports. They are important both in their own right (possibly 5 to 7 percent of the NAC Gross Domestic Product) and because of their role in oiling the wheels of the competitive market economy. Financial services have not benefited to the same extent as manufactured goods in progress toward dismantling barriers to trade between Mexico, Canada, and the United States, but it is clear that the benefits of a unified market should apply in the financial services sector as much as any other.

A general approach on financial services must be closely linked to the program of liberalization of capital movements, as a result of which residents of any NAC nation will have access to the financial systems of other NAC countries and all the financial products which are available there. Equally, there should be no restrictions on capital transfers and no discrimination in the form of fiscal measures. A program in the financial services sector purports to break down national regulatory barriers that obstruct freedom of establishment and free trade in services that could continue even after exchange controls are fully removed. A unified banking system is needed where a bank can establish branches anywhere in the NAC and offer its services throughout its territories; an insurance market where insurance can be bought on the most competitive terms and provide NAC-wide coverage; and a securities and capital market with enough capacity to meet the continent's financing needs and be capable of attracting investors from around the globe.

The general method of achieving full freedom of establishment and free trade in financial services can be summarized as:

—the standardization of essential standards for prudential supervision of financial institutions and for the protection of investors, depositors, and consumers

—mutual recognition of the competence of the supervisory bodies and standards of each NAC country

—based on the first two points, home country control and supervision of financial institutions for those who wish to operate in another NAC country.

The Movement of Goods and People

The transport market is characterized at the international level by quotas and other restrictions. The costs to importers and exporters that arise from insufficient competition in this market impede the growth and integration of the NAC economy. To remedy this unsatisfactory situation and give NAC suppliers and users of transport services a genuine common market, the NAC must adopt a two-phase approach applicable to the main transport sectors, road, sea, and air. In the first phase, the objective is to liberalize transport services between nations of the NAC. In the second phase, the objective is to liberalize transport within nations of the NAC by opening up the national markets to non-resident carriers.

Any adoption of such measures will permit the elimination of the border control of the current bilateral quotas in transport and the possibility for a transport carrier to operate in any NAC nation, either occasionally or on a permanent basis.

Keeping Pace with New Technologies

In this field, the challenge confronting the NAC is that of creating a unified market for those services which are linked to rapidly changing innovative technology. Regulations are needed for cross-border broadcasting and information services, as well as standards for advanced equipment. The fragmentation of NAC nations into separate national markets as a result of varying technical requirements reduces the scope for economies of scale, multiplies the costs of obtaining type approvals, and renders less attractive research on a scale sufficient to sustain the hemisphere's competitiveness in international markets.

A Well-Trained Workforce

The NAC, especially the northern hemisphere, has already achieved movement in this field, particularly in the case of employees. However, there remain a number of problems to be solved if the internal market in goods and services is to be matched by efficiency in the allocation of labor and competition in professional services.

On the one hand, there are general obstacles such as the taxation problems faced by border workers and the administrative problems faced by nonemployed citizens of a NAC country who wish to take up residence in another NAC country. On the other hand, there are obstacles specific to certain regulated professions. These involve the recognition of foreign qualifications. NAC must tackle these obstacles in one of two ways:

—standardization of professional training, as with the medical professions, who have the right to establish and practice these services throughout the NAC because of standardized educational systems

—through a general system of mutual recognition by the nations of the NAC of each other's higher education diplomas.

BANKING

An absolute precondition for an open NAC market in banking services is that money should be able to move freely across the New American Community nations. NAC governments will be asked to respect each other's interpretation of those rules and to allow financial firms to sell in each other's markets whatever they can sell in the home country and under control from home. This goes beyond national treatment. For example, a U.S. bank behaves in Mexico like a Mexican bank and vice versa. Mutual recognition of rules is equivalent to a far tougher trade demand, equivalent access. It gives a branch of a U.S. bank the right to do in Mexico what it is allowed to do in the United States. This will result in a single license allowing a bank to open in all NAC nations or to provide services across frontiers as a matter of right. Each branch in the NAC will be supervised by authorities in the head office nation.

All nations in the NAC regulate access to their banking system and supervise its operations, but controls differ. A bank based in one country wishing to establish branches in the others currently needs authorization from different supervising authorities, each with their own conditions for granting authorization and for subsequent supervision.

To overcome these obstacles a three-faceted strategy is needed:

—essential standardization of law and practice across the NAC nations for capital requirements, standards of experience and repute for management, monitoring solvency and liquidity, prevention of over-lending to individual borrowers, forms and contents of published accounts
—mutual recognition by the national supervisory authorities of the controls operated by each other will follow this standardization, and
—home country control through coordination of national supervisory activities will mean that a bank operating in another NAC country will be controlled by the authorities in its home base.

At the heart of these proposals is the single banking license enabling banks licensed in one country to establish branches and provide cross-border services throughout the NAC. Licenses for banks based outside the NAC will be based on the principle of reciprocity. The non-NAC bank will have similar rights within the NAC to those enjoyed by NAC-based banks operating in that non-member nation.

Regulations in banking deal with two types of institutions. The business of a credit institution is to receive deposits from the public and to grant credit on its own account. If an institution is not a credit institution, but its principle activity is to grant credit or make investments, it is a financial institution.

Consequently, new regulations in banking are needed:

—to define certain specialized credit institutions which are exempt from this approach
—to promote a unified market for banking through sufficient standardization of essential supervisory rules, which will support mutual recognition of each national supervisory authority's competence and rules, which will in turn result

in home country control by the supervisory authority in the home NAC nation. This will enable a bank authorized in one country to operate in all the others without further authorization in the latter

—to standardize the format and contents of the published accounts of banks and other financial institutions. As more credit institutions operate across national borders within the NAC, it is becoming increasingly important that their accounts are comparable

—to remove the need for foreign branches of banks and other financial institutions to publish separate annual accounts so that they are treated the same way as branches of domestic financial institutions

—to lay down measures concerning the reorganization and winding-up of credit institutions operating in several NAC nations. This is entrusted to the competent authorities of the NAC nation in which the credit institution has its head office. In the case of credit institutions having their head office outside the NAC the authorities of the host nation would be responsible, unless there is a bilateral agreement with the home nation, for laying down transitional measures concerning deposit guarantee schemes in order to extend their coverage. Deposit guarantee schemes provide protection for a depositor if the credit institution becomes bankrupt

—to lay down common standards for the "own funds" of authorized credit institutions for the purpose of supervision by the regulatory authorities. "Own funds" are the funds that are the property of the bank, as opposed to "client funds," which are on deposit with the bank but the property of the clients. The size of own funds is used by regulatory bodies in calculating acceptable levels of lending. Standardization of these calculations throughout the NAC is essential for mutual recognition of home country control

—to lay down standardized minimum requirements for deposit guarantee schemes and encourage the introduction of such schemes by all NAC nations. These schemes provide protection for the depositor if the credit institution becomes bankrupt. Such requirements stimulate NAC countries without deposit guarantee schemes to set them up. Deposit guarantee schemes should contain measures for winding-up of credit institutions to give cross-border coverage

—to promote the standardization of the supervision of large exposures, say, where a large proportion of the loans of a credit institution are to a single client or group of related clients

—to remove obstacles to the provision of mortgage credit across borders and to improve the cooperation between supervisory bodies in NAC nations

—to standardize solvency ratios.

Certainly one of the most debatable issues, filled with emotion and misperception, will be the evolution of a single banking currency and a central NAC Bank. Within the NAC, fears and promises surrounding the sovereignty question may encourage a truly integrated forum that should be welcomed and participated in by all interested and appropriate parties. The decision on one currency and one banking authority cuts to the heart of services that will dictate the future direction and its acceptance by the majority within the NAC.

INSURANCE

NAC member nations will have the right to set up branches in other NAC nations. Consideration must be made of whether they be permitted active or passive insurance sales. For example, a Canadian customer would be allowed to buy life insurance in Mexico on his or her own initiative, but the Mexican insurer would only be allowed to market its policies in Canada under Canadian rules and supervision. Nations of the NAC already possess a body of legislation coordinating national laws on the establishment and operation of insurance companies. These coordinated laws cover aspects such as the initial setting up of an insurance business and the opening of branches and agencies, as well as subsequent supervision of, for example, technical reserves, assets, solvency margins, and minimum guarantee funds.

A number of obstacles remain to the freedom of an insurance company established in one nation of the NAC to cover risks situated in other NAC nations. In common with other financial services, the general method for achieving freedom of establishment and trade should be:

—standardization of essential standards for supervision

—mutual recognition by the national supervisory authorities of the controls operated by each other

—home country control through coordination of national supervisory activities. This will mean that any insurance company operating in other NAC countries will be controlled by the authorities in its home base, except for consumer protection, in specified cases.

The proposals distinguish between mass risk and large risk insurance. Mass risk applies to policies for individuals while large risk applies to large firms. The distinction will be determined by the value of the insurance coverage being obtained. National supervision and control is particularly important for ensuring consumer protection in mass risk business. This will necessitate some limited retention of host country control. This approach will remove the remaining obstacles to the provision of insurance services across borders while maintaining appropriate levels of supervision and protection of policyholders. Regulations needed in insurance include:

—to standardize annual accounts of insurance companies in different NAC countries so they become comparable, thus contributing to a single unified insurance market

—to standardize NAC nations' provisions concerning the compulsory winding-up of insurance firms

—to promote the cross-border provision of non-life insurance by coordinating laws concerning information in policies, coverage, premiums, and the obligations of policy holders and insurers

—to open up the various national markets so that insurance firms will have more freedom to conduct non-life business across borders and to ensure an appropriate level of supervision of insurance companies so that consumers are adequately protected

—to coordinate national requirements for insurance against legal costs

—to provide adequate financial guarantees for credit insurance

—to outline procedures for freedom to supply motor liability insurance services

—to outline procedures for freedom to suppy life insurance services.

SECURITIES

If the NAC is to become a unified market, as opposed to a group of national markets, a NAC securities market system must be created to meet the needs of both investors and companies who go to the markets for capital and borrowings. Financial intermediaries authorized in one nation shall be able to operate throughout the NAC on the basis of a single license given in their home country.

The general approach to achieving the single securities market is common to that adopted in all areas of financial services. The three-faceted approach consists of agreement on essential standards, mutual recognition by the national supervisory authorities of the controls operated by each other in their home bases, and home country control, though coordination of national supervisory authorities will mean that any organization operating in several countries of the NAC will be controlled by the authorities in its home base.

The NAC must coordinate the conditions for admission of securities to official stock exchange listing, the contents, scrutiny, and method of publication of the listing particulars, and the publication of information by quoted firms. An NAC system requires additional action on further aspects of the securities markets.

Regulations needed in the securities area include:

—to specify which authorities should check and approve stock-exchange particulars in cases where application for listing is made in more than one country. To provide for reciprocal agreements with non-NAC nations

—to ensure adequate provision of information concerning securities and their issuers. To provide for mutual recognition of prospectuses approved in a single NAC nation

—to coordinate policy on investor protection with regard to publication of information about major share holdings

—to define and prohibit insider dealings

—to coordinate national laws governing unit trust to give unit holders throughout the NAC uniform and more effective protection. To permit these firms to market units throughout the NAC on the basis of a single license

—to enable unit trust and comparable bodies to treat certain privately issued bonds as offering similar security to state guaranteed bonds

—to evolve standards on investment services.

TRANSPORT

The right to provide transport services freely throughout the NAC is an essential element of the transport policy. Transport within NAC is bedevilled by quotas, restrictions, and limits on access to the market. These restrict competition in the NAC, increase costs for trade across internal borders, and impede the integration of a NAC economy.

There should be two phases involved in dealing with transport issues: firstly, liberalizing transport services between NAC nations; secondly, liberalizing transport within NAC nations by opening up the national markets to non-resident carriers. The various transport markets involved are:

—road transport sector where non-resident carriers should be given the freedom to supply goods and passenger transport services within the NAC while quotas for the international carriage of goods should be phased out

—inland waterways sector where the international transport of goods and passengers should be liberalized and conditions established for non-resident carriers to operate services within NAC nations

—maritime transport sector where NAC shipping firms will be free from restrictions on the supply of services between ports within NAC nations and between NAC nations and third countries

—air transport sector where increased competition in services and fares should be introduced while the rights of governments to restrict capacity and access to markets should be limited.

Regulations needed in transport include:

—to move toward common road transport markets between NAC nations, at the same time ensuring the implementation of freedom to provide services, the abolition of unnecessary and costly restrictions, fair competition, and minimum disturbance to the market

—to realize the freedom to provide services by setting out the conditions under which non-resident carriers will be permitted to carry out national road haulage services

—to establish common rules governing the international carriage of passengers by road and to facilitate border crossing

—to enable non-resident carriers to have the freedom to provide national passenger transport services within a NAC country

—to lay down the conditions under which non-resident carriers may have freedom to operate inland waterways transport services within a NAC nation

—to ensure the freedom of NAC nations to provide maritime transport services in trade to and from NAC and to safeguard fair competition

—to promote greater competition and efficiency in the air transport sector by improving access to routes and regulating arrangements for capacity sharing

—to extend the network of air services within the NAC by giving air carriers greater scope to develop services between regions in different NAC countries. This should encourage further development of scheduled international services between a regional airport and either a second regional airport or a major airport

—to establish more flexible arrangements for approving scheduled passenger air fares between NAC countries and settling disputes rapidly. This will enable NAC countries to move toward a single market in air transport

—to introduce greater competition into the air transport industry. This should evolve gradually in order to avoid disruption. However, this balance will most benefit the consumer

—to provide appropriate procedures, powers, and penalties to ensure compliance in the air transport sector with competition rules

—to standardize and provide procedures in air services and fares, passenger capacity, and market access

—to standardize air crew qualifications.

NEW TECHNOLOGIES AND SERVICES

Rapidly changing innovative information technologies have given rise to a range of new information services. These play an increasingly significant role in the economy, and have potential for considerable cross-border development. It is vital that one strong unified market is created for these new services, rather than letting them evolve to differing technical standards in a number of fragmented, national markets. The NAC market will benefit users of these services by increasing choice and competition. It will benefit the suppliers by providing economies of scale in research, development, and type approval and by increasing NAC competitiveness in global markets.

To achieve this, nations of the western hemisphere will have to dismantle the obstacles which constrain the cross-border supply of these new information services. It also has to solve problems caused by the differing technical standards of the equipment used. Regulations needed in the new technologies and services area include:

—to ensure that all residents in the NAC have access to all NAC broadcasts which have become possible with satellite and cable technology. To remove the obstacles to this which result from NAC nations' rules on copyright, advertising, and protection of children

—to create better market conditions for the accelerated development of information services aimed at professionals in research, trade, and industry. The main goals are to stimulate and reinforce the competitive capabilities of NAC information suppliers, to promote the use of advanced information services in the NAC and to set up an internal information service market

—to aim for standardization in the development of payment card systems. This will allow for inter-operability between the different networks and thus ensure equal access for all card holders to all distribution networks. This should contribute to the rapid modernization of banking services, distribution and telecommunication services throughout the NAC. It will also aid the free movement of goods and capital

—to produce common technical specifications for direct satellite broadcasting of television programs and their redistribution by cable. This will establish common standards for the production of television sets and allow programs to be received throughout the NAC

—to promote closer cooperation in establishing NAC technical standards in the information technology and telecommunications sectors

—to promote NAC capability to produce telecommunications equipment through the mutual recognition by NAC nations of type approvals

—to promote the development of NAC land-based cellular communications by ensuring the free movement of mobile telephones through NAC, the compatibility of networks, and NAC standards for manufacture.

CAPITAL MOVEMENTS

A single market in which goods, services, and persons circulate freely can only function efficiently if the related capital movements are unrestricted. In order to complete a unified market, restrictions on capital transfers must be abolished, and residents of any NAC nation must have free access to the financial systems and products of other NAC nations. Regulations needed in the capital movements area are:

—to remove remaining restrictions on capital movements between NAC nations as part of the completion of an internal market. This is a primary step in setting up an efficient, stable and attractive NAC financial system

—to complete the effective liberalization throughout the NAC of the capital operations directly necessary for the proper functioning of the common market and for the linkage of domestic capital markets. This would liberalize cross-border movements relating to the admission of securities to the capital markets, transactions in securities not dealt in on a stock exchange, long-term commerical loans, and on unit trusts.

FREE MOVEMENT OF LABOR AND THE PROFESSIONS

One of the fundamental principles of any successful hemispheric agreement would permit a person from any NAC country to be free to live and work in another NAC nation as an employee or to be self-employed. This ultimately would produce a free movement of labor and professions.

Regulations needed in the area of the free movement of labor and the professions include:

—to harmonize income taxes and certain tax reliefs for non-resident workers

—to remove obstacles to the free movement of non-employed people

—to promote the mutual recognition by NAC nations of higher education qualifications and the right of those so qualified to practice their professional skills

—to establish comparability of vocational training qualifications throughout the NAC nations. This would allow workers to practice their skills throughout the entire NAC

—to strengthen cooperation between industry and training institutions in order to improve the initial training and updating of skills for those whose employment is affected by technological innovations

—to promote a unified market for technical research and consultancy by adopting transitional arrangements for the mutual recognition by NAC nations of technical qualifications and practice experience

—to adopt transitional measures for recognition of diplomas in the field of engineering

—to define the minimum range of activities which formally qualified pharmacists can pursue in all NAC nations. To set up an advisory committee on pharmaceutical training

—to facilitate the right to set up practice as a pharmacist in any NAC nation

—to provide for the specific training of general medical practitioners, allowing mutual recognition of medical qualifications throughout NAC

—to coordinate national legislation concerning relationships between self-employed commercial agents and their principles.

The list of services appears endless, as it assuredly is. It goes beyond the above to include cultural, historic, language, artistic, and religious considerations. The complexities are considerable as additional countries are invited to join the NAC. Each nation, possessing differing expressions of service for its population, will be forced to reexamine and often surrender traditional schemes in favor of those regulated by the NAC. The fullness of people's everyday experiences need to be reevaluated as they will be altered once the NAC sets its goals and borders are opened. There is much to gain from releasing services, enriching all along the way.

15

JOINT RESEARCH, DEVELOPMENT, AND TECHNOLOGY

No one can doubt the importance and urgency of cooperation in research among nations. By implementing a substantial research and technology policy, the NAC can complement and integrate the efforts being made at national levels. The NAC should ensure that all significant intellectual and financial resources available within the boundaries of her nations are used in a rational manner, avoiding unnecessary duplication. Needless to say, all findings and applications require an open and full sharing with participants.

THE JAPANESE MODEL

In other industrial nations, combined efforts are moving forward. In Japan there is the immensely successful Ministry of International Trade and Industry. MITI spends 0.26 percent of Japan's gross national product in basic research, nearly as much as the United States. Most Japanese policy is dealt with in each of the numerous ministries, and what passes for government policy is really an assortment of individual decisions, moved upward for information, and finally for approval. MITI can decide that a specific branch of industry, for example, steel, computers, or bicycles, should be developed and initiate appropriate strategies to accomplish that goal. It then selects those projects and firms, searches for proper financing, and makes recommendations.

To enhance Japanese industry, a primary objective of MITI has been to encourage growth and concentration of companies, which led the Japanese Fair Trade Commission to claim 158 cases of violation of their antimonopology law in 1976 and 171 in 1977. MITI is one of the major sponsors of official Japanese cartels, to promote production or prevent an economic downturn. One of MITI's first objectives derived from a March 1980 document showing that during the 1970s Japan had become a major economic force whose behavior impacted on the rest of the globe. Three national goals for the new decade were spelled out: increased international contributions; the reduction of resource dependency; and the development of private-sector vitality and the improvement of the quality of life in Japan.

Then in early 1986 another MITI publication outlined strategies for Japan as it moved toward the year 2000. New structures were identified as: the contribution of the structures to the international economy and community; changes in domestic economic factors; and new lifestyles. MITI encouraged the government to shift from export-led to domestic demand-led growth as a key element of the internationalization of Japan. MITI had become Japan's primary industrial goal-setter and influenced significantly the country's economic growth. It carefully supervised the acquisition of foreign technology via licensing agreements with other nations, established foreign exchange controls, and arranged that the best of technology be secured under the most advantageous terms by those individuals and/or firms who are best positioned to use it.

MITI became the omnipotent regulator of production and distribution of goods and services in Japan. It designed and orchestrated the nation's direction and structure for her industry. In all, six functions evolved for MITI: to be responsible for the control of Japan's foreign trade and to oversee international commerce; guaranteeing the smooth flow of goods in the national economy; acquiring jurisdictional control over manufacturing, mining, and distribution firms and being responsible for promoting their evolution; acquiring for Japan a reliable and continuing supply of raw materials and energy resources; managing the government's policies toward small firms; and encouraging and mapping strategies for the nation's smaller companies.

The first three are primary concerns for MITI as the ministry controls international trade, regulates the production and distribution of goods, and prepares Japan's industry for future challenges. As described by Michio Morishima in his 1982 book, *Why Has Japan Succeeded?*:

In sectors of policy interest, MITI collects a good deal of market and competitive data, gives administrative guidance to firms, and issues a lot of paper in support of a policy. Communication between MITI and individual producers takes place frequently at several levels. Some observers of this process have mistakenly concluded that MITI is dictating investment rates in the industry. This is not

MITI's intention. Market prospects, not ministries, stimulate investment in growth businesses and ultimately discourage investment in declining ones. MITI understands that it would be counterproductive to force wary producers to invest. Nor can a ministry know any particular business sector well enough to design or direct a specific series of investments. Instead, MITI tries to develop a shared perception of a business' future and designs incentives and subsidies to accelerate the desired course.

MITI's primary enforcement tool is "administrative guidance," a form of carrot and stick maneuver. This strategy is employed in MITI's three broad industrial policy concerns: investment rate and structure of producers, technology development, and export-import measures. When a specific industry is expanding rapidly, MITI urges the industry to consolidate, for example, by merging into one. When an industry is declining, MITI urges capacity retirement. In this way MITI purports to accelerate market forces and create more stable competition among a few relatively low-cost manufacturers.

By year's end 1986, a new recommendation surfaced encouraging Japan to foster domestic growth in a way that would aid the international community at the same time encouraging free trade, especially with other Asian nations and other developing nations.

As globalization further encroached on Japanese manufacturing by the end of the 1980s, MITI had to redefine its mission, which had focused on domestic matters, and probably surrender a significant portion of its former power. Every three or four years MITI presents its "Visions," which are sweeping examinations of major world trends and how they impact on Japan. These reports are legitimized by recommendations fed back to them by an Industrial Structure Council. And MITI, shrouded in mystery, continues to send shivers down the back of world executives and government officials also responsible for industry, research, and development within their own nations, forever trying to figure out why and how Japan has been so successful with her Ministry of International Trade and Industry.

Although impressive and related to future domination, Japan's Ministry of International Trade and Industry is an inadequate model for the NAC because MITI talks of the efforts of a single nation, while NAC has multiple states that must interact in R & D programs. In addition, the entire cultural history of Japan is too different from the U.S. and other western hemispheric traditions, experiences, and preferred style. It is from Europe, and in particular the European Community, that we will prosper most by studying her impressive strides recently taken in the research and development arena with cooperation among its 12 partners.

THE EUROPEAN COMMUNITY MODEL

As described in the opening chapter, the European Community's best kept secret is her most threatening weapon. The E.C. and member governments are releasing billions of dollars for their megaresearch programs. Within the next six years, along with company resources, about $16 billion will be used to develop high-tech research and their resulting offsprings of products. With new E.C. directives, revised tax laws will allow greater expansion into the venture capital markets, resulting in Europe surpassing the $2.5 billion the U.S. spent in 1988.

The E.C. is combining people, talents, ambitions, and resources to assert its determined leadership in science and technology. So must we. In each case the persuasive efforts of the European Community are worthy of careful examination by the NAC, as we find here, more than with the Japanese model. NAC can capture much of these united efforts, both in reducing wasteful repetition and ultimately in providing a more open society of futuristic opportunities.

A RESPONSE—ACTION WITH ACCOUNTABILITY

Of course, so much of Europe and Japan's R&D programs have been initially modeled after those of the United States, especially within the European Community, that it would seem that emulation of these strategies suggests that we would be copying ourselves. Not necessarily. To begin with, much time has passed since these original U.S. models were used by other laboratories' researchers. These dedicated and talented people have carefully weighed our approaches with deep commitment and experimentation and drawn from our best, with the elimination of shortfalls. We should now consider doing the same, by borrowing and reexamining that which was developed in other industrialized nations around the globe, responding in kind with a super-program that is both productive, disciplined, accountable, and cost effective.

There is both hope and opportunity ahead. Spending on R&D in the U.S. almost equals the combined spending of Germany and Japan, with Britain and France included. American industries are typically larger— the U.S. economy is about four times Germany's and twice Japan's. And big economies do not have to spend much more on research and development than smaller economies to generate equal advances in productivity. An innovation can cut costs by 10 percent whether an industry is big or small.

Initially, the United States will dominate most efforts as we possess the capability unlike that of others within the NAC. But we should encourage shifts as the comparative advantage of transferring some of our efforts to other nations would more than offset losses within our borders. Rather than test the reader with a parallel listing of research, development, and technology projects that the NAC might entertain, it would be best to merely list those areas where continued work is needed.

Quality of Life

—Health—Essential to the quality of life is the level of human well-being, and research into areas relevant to the solution of major health problems should be carried out in the NAC. One of the primary concerns should be the impact of modern technologies on human health, and one of the specific aims should be to reduce health risks and improve the prevention of accidents in industrial sectors such as coal mining, iron and steel production, and construction. Medical research programs should be carried out through the coordination of national research efforts, enabling the financial resources and capabilities available to member nations to be used as effectively as possible. A program should cover a wide range of subjects including environmental and lifestyle-related health problems and age-related diseases and disabilities.

—Environment—Pollution knows no boundaries, and if there is any field which requires international cooperation it is environmental protection. The NAC must develop a comprehensive and coherent environmental policy based on a major research effort in the environmental field. Indeed, only research can provide the knowledge needed to prepare new regulations and to improve the technical means of preventing and correcting the adverse effects of human activities on the environment.

Information Technology and Telecommunications

—Information technologies—Information technologies and their applications have become a determining factor in industrial competitiveness and constitute one of the fastest growing economic sectors. By the end of this century, and well into the early portion of the new millennium, information technologies will be the most important manufacturing sector in the world economy, and it is vital that the NAC put as much effort into this field as the other major industrial powers. The soaring cost of developing information technologies, and the need to create a continental-scale market in order to recoup the cost, require a long-term research strategy based on NAC cooperation.

—Telecommunications—In a world where 65 percent of economic activity is linked to information to one degree or another, the development of more efficient ways to transmit data is a factor which determines progress. Telecommunications is not only a major force behind technological development and a critical source of new jobs, it also absorbs a great deal of public and private investment. Telecommunications are inherently international. If the best use is to be made of their potential, and duplication is to be avoided, the countries of the NAC must coordinate their efforts.

Industrial Technologies

—Industrial technologies—The spectacular progress made by information technology and biotechnology must not be allowed to overshadow the importance of technology, research, and development in the more traditional industrial sectors such as motor vehicles, chemicals, textiles, and construction. This is essential since it is the only means of developing new products and processes. Innovation often consists of adapting recent developments in other fields to the particular requirements of those industries. In each case a wide range of new technologies is providing scope for profound changes in those sectors.

—Advanced materials—Another factor that greatly affects technological progress is the existence of suitable materials. NAC nations must maintain a position which is essential to progress in electronics, data processing, telecommunications, the motor industry, ship building, construction, aerospace, biomedical technologies, and other sectors.

—Raw materials—The NAC's research into raw materials should cover three different sectors, each of which is important to her economy. The first is metals and minerals, and research in this area should be aimed at increasing the discovery of deep or hidden underground deposits in member nations by improving prospecting techniques and by upgrading mining technology and ore treatment processes. The purpose of this research should be to strengthen the competitive position of the extractive and metals industries in nations of the NAC by reducing her vulnerability regarding a number of strategic raw materials.

—Steel—Steel is still one of the most important of the traditional industrial sectors. Programs must be developed to encourage technical research in order to boost the competitiveness of the steel-producing and steel-using industries in the NAC.

—Industrial Norms and Standards—Throughout the NAC there must be industrial norms and standards. This in turn calls for a certain amount of specialized research which, owing to the need for neutrality and objectivity, is a NAC task par excellence. Standardization throughout the NAC is essential.

Energy

—Thermonuclear fusion—Thermonuclear fusion offers the possibility of a new form of power generation using a virtually inexhaustive source of fuel, and with only a limited impact on the environment. Nuclear fusion reactions are the same as those by which the sun produces the energy it radiates. The elements involved are in plentiful supply throughout the universe. In order to exploit such reactions in a controlled way on earth, those elements must be raised to temperatures of the order of 100 million degrees centigrade.

—Nuclear fission—Until the day when fusion energy becomes commercially viable, nuclear fission will continue to play a major role in supplying the NAC's energy needs. However, the use of such energy requires that the necessary precautions are taken to safeguard the environment and human health. Therefore the NAC's activities in the nuclear fission field should be focused on the problems of nuclear safety.

—Non-nuclear energy—The NAC should be keen to make the best use of all energy sources available to it by maintaining a diversified technological capacity within the NAC, by conducting research in the broad field of non-nuclear energy (fossil fuels), and the rational use of energy.

Biotechnologies and Agriculture

—Biotechnologies—Biotechnologies are the techniques and processes which make use of the properties of living organisms for agricultural, industrial, or medical purposes. Since the identification, 30 years ago, of the structure of DNA and the genetic code, knowledge has advanced rapidly under the pressure of international competition.

—Agriculture—Agriculture is an area of active research to provide a strong back-up to industrial work, dealing with soil, modern methods of production, preservation, and processing and their effects on the quality of foodstuffs, and the feeding, genetics, and diseases of cattle.

The New American Community for Researchers

—Stimulating cooperation and exchanges—Nations of the NAC have a significant and high-level human research potential which is largely used in a less-than-optimal way because of institutional rigidity and the existence of national barriers. Making researchers more mobile and offering them opportunities for international and interdisciplinary contacts are simple ways of improving the results obtained from NAC research to an extent that has proved to be spectacular.

—Development Aid—The NAC should work actively in promoting the use of science and technology to help solve problems in the Third World. By encouraging cooperation between scientists from the NAC and colleagues in the Third World it also fosters closer ties with developing nations.

—International Cooperation—International cooperation with non-NAC nations is critical in evolving a sound research and technology policy. Links must be expanded throughout the industrial and non-industrialized world through specific bilateral agreements covering scientific and technical cooperation, or by general framework agreements incorporating a scientific or technical section.

New American Community taxpayers in the United States, and to a lesser extent in Canada may well cry foul. For decades, minimal expenditures have been made in Spanish and Portuguese speaking nations. Why suddenly share expertise with the newcomers who appear to have all to gain with little to offer in exchange? In the spirit of the NAC, this attitude must dissolve. Should each layer of input be thus weighed, no integrated common market could ever evolve. Some tradeoffs are always needed, some gains are shared by the mighty with the less competent, experienced, or trained. The shoe may someday shift to the other foot. Lest we forget, nations south of the United States are rich in many ways, a work ethic, natural resources, an abundance of manpower, and an untested will to achieve.

The New American Community's involvement in research and technology has two beneficial effects: valuable results in the form of advances in scientific knowledge or technological processes, and the development of a genuine tradition of collaborative research involving close, frequent, and long-term cooperation between research centers, universities, and firms in each of the member nations. Individually, countries of the New American Community have made significant contributions. Combined efforts via the NAC will provide the encouragement needed to continue these, and other expanded tasks which, though progressing well, will prosper in the process of building a genuine NAC research and technology community.

16

A STANDARDS POLICY

Differing technical regulations and national standards in the NAC's nations are a very real obstacle to the creation of an effective and unified hemispheric market. The effects are widespread, adding real costs and wasting valuable resources, restricting consumer choice and impeding the NAC's full competitive potential.

The existence of different technical regulations in individual NAC nations forces manufacturers to concentrate on national rather than NAC-wide markets. It is necessary to have different production lines for the different nations, and so the opportunities to reap economies of scale are reduced. As a result, costs are higher (often as much as 10 percent of total product costs). Within the E.C., for example, the existence of separate national testing and type-approval procedures for telephone switchboards means that costs are 8 percent higher than in the U.S.

These barriers result from differences between NAC nations in three types of arrangements:

—technical regulations lay down the legal requirements enacted by the national parliaments mainly in the interests of health and safety and the environment. Often these regulations refer to standards:
—standards are produced by private national standardization bodies. While they are only voluntary codes they often assume a quasi-legal status because of their use as a reference in technical regulations or insurance claims;
—type testing and certification is used to check that a product complies either with voluntary standards or with statutory regulation. A typical problem is that

one nation does not recognize another's type test, thus causing the costs and delays of additional testing.

Unless monitored, unified standards can potentially lead to a form of protectionism by:

—the habit of writing product regulations in terms of the ends (the machine should not catch fire even at full power) rather than the means (use the following fireproofing techniques) remains hard to instill.

—the existence of a basic NAC regulation for a product does not necessarily give it a passport across the NAC.

—the certification system allowing manufacturers to demonstrate that their products meet NAC safety rules is inadequate.

—setting standards for products continues to create problems.

The E.C.'s experiences, the most parallel to those of a NAC, are worth examining. The original approach to dismantling these barriers was to attempt to standardize national regulations across the Community. However, this proved a very difficult and protracted process; the relevant technology had sometimes even changed by the time that eventual agreement was reached. (It is said that the E.C. took more than a decade to decide what is an appropriate jar label for marmalade.) At the same time, increased concern for health, safety, and the environment, and the rapid growth in technical innovation was multiplying the occasions on which differences in national approaches and regulations were occurring.

The New American Community's response to standardization should revolve around: minimum standardization of member nations' regulations; the creation of standardized NAC requirements by NAC standardization bodies; as a transition measure, mutual recognition of national standards until appropriate NAC standards are created.

A NEW APPROACH TO STANDARDIZATION

The problems caused by the existence of different technical regulations and national standards within the NAC nations have been recognized for many years and some progress has been made in the elimination of such barriers to trade vis-à-vis free-trade accords.

To move toward the goal of removing technical barriers to trade, a new approach to standardization is called for, which should be based on the following principles:

—a distinction will be drawn in future internal market initiatives between what is essential to standardize legislation and what may be left to be standardized by hemisphere bodies.

—legislative standardization will in the future be restricted to laying down health, safety, and other essential requirements.

—industrial standardization will be achieved by the elaboration of standards throughout the Americas. As a transitional measure, and insofar as standardized procedures do not yet exist, national standards may be recognized as equivalent through an appropriate procedure by an authorized body of the NAC. The result will be that a product manufactured in one NAC country in conformity with NAC legislation as regards its essential safety requirements and with a standard in other respects will be guaranteed automatic access to the markets of all other NAC nations.

Regulations needed in the standardized policy area are many but include:

—to inform an authorized body of NAC of new standards and regulations from any NAC nation in certain fields prior to their enactment. The NAC body should be empowered to freeze the introduction of these new national regulations for up to a time period, perhaps a year, if it is decided that they should be replaced by a NAC initiative (in order to prevent new barriers to free-trade being created). This would extend the coverage of legislation to a wider range of products.

—to ensure a minimum level of safety throughout the NAC nations for pressure vessels. The standardization of safety procedures will also aid the free movement of such products. In addition, a universally recognized testing procedure and mark of conformity will prevent wasteful checks being carried out in each NAC nation.

—to standardize the safety regulations on toys throughout the Community in order to protect children's health and facilitate trade; to introduce an NAC mark to show that a toy conforms to the required safety standards.

—to standardize national laws concerning the responsibility for ensuring health and safety of people using machinery. Presently, NAC countries have existing national legislation to ensure the health and safety of workers and other people using hazardous machinery.

—to standardize national provision on permissible electromagnetic disturbance and immunity levels caused by electronic apparatus in order to guarantee the free movement of these goods.

MOTOR VEHICLES

The NAC should strive to bring about a comprehensive NAC type-approval for passenger cars. This would allow a car approved in one NAC nation to be marketed in another without having to obtain new type-approval, for example, for tire size, content of gasoline, or vehicle size, which is wasteful, costly, and time-consuming.

Regulations needed in the motor vehicles area are many but might include:

—to abolish existing national type-approvals for motor vehicles and trailers and replace them with one NAC-wide type-approval. This will simplify the administrative burden for the industry and facilitate the free circulation and use of motor vehicles.

—to standardize the different national type-approvals for motor vehicles related to permissible weights and dimensions.

—to bring into line the different national type-approvals for tires for motor vehicles and their trailers.

—NAC nations currently have a variety of national type-approvals for safety glass used in motor vehicles. To introduce a single NAC type-approval for vehicle safety glass, so as to promote the single market for motor vehicles. The use of laminated glass is mandatory (rather than the use of the less safe toughened glass).

—to regulate the permissible sound level of motorcycle exhaust systems. To bring existing national type-approval for motorcycle exhaust systems closer together and to include replacement of exhaust systems within its scope.

—to reduce car pollution in order to avoid adverse effects such as acid rain. Technical specifications are needed to permit the use of lead-free gasoline.

—to approximate the technical requirements of diesel vehicle engines with the NAC nations to combat gaseous pollution and promote the free movement of goods.

—to reduce air pollution by gases from motor vehicles below 1400 cc.

—to reduce particulate emissions from diesel engines.

—to bring national provisions relating to tire pressure gauges, including technical specification, closer together so as to facilitate intra-NAC nation trade in these products.

TRACTORS AND AGRICULTURAL MACHINERY

The existence of differing national product regulations and standards is a major problem in the manufacture of agricultural machinery. Production lines cannot be centralized, which prevents manufacturers from taking advantage of economies of scale. A further problem is the absence of NAC-wide type-approval procedures. Individual NAC nations thus require national testing and certification for components, a costly and wasteful process.

Regulations needed in the tractors and agricultural machinery area are many but include:

—to standardize the technical requirements of tractors in all NAC nations, to promote type-approval procedures and to promote free trade within the NAC nations.

—to give to an authoritative NAC body powers to update legislation on type-approval of tractors, as new technologies are often appearing.

—to standardize the technical requirements for front mounted roll-over protection structures on narrow track tractors. This will improve safety and also ensure that the NAC type-approval procedure can be uniformly applied throughout the NAC, allowing reciprocal recognition of testing procedures in all NAC nations.

FOOD

One of the fundamental principles of the NAC should be the free movement of goods. Any national measure which hinders intra-NAC trade should be denied. No national law should prevent the marketing of a product lawfully produced and marketed in another NAC country. This means mutual recognition by the hemispheric nations of each other's product standards.

However, this legal principle does not eliminate all practical difficulties for exporting manufacturers. Individual nations can still maintain separate laws for the protection of public health and consumer interests. Clearly, such rules cannot always be easily applied to a given set of circumstances. NAC-level standardization of regulations in these areas is necessary.

A genuine common market for food requires an updated, new strategy uniting sufficient standardization of national regulations and procedures to protect public health, provide consumers with clear labelling and protection in matters other than health, ensure fair trading, and provide for the necessary public controls.

In all other respects, there should be mutual recognition of each NAC nation's regulations and standards, so that a product acceptable for sale in one country should be acceptable throughout the NAC.

This new approach would be implemented in the first instance by a framework of horizontal regulations which lay down the philosophy and controls for a particular area, for example, additives. Regulations would be complemented by specific horizontal regulations detailing how these requirements are to be applied to specific segments of a wider area, for example, flavorings as a category of additives. In addition, there is a need for commodity or product regulations on certain types of foods.

Regulations needed in the food area are many but a few examples include:

—to ensure that the free movement of food within the NAC is not compromised by different national regulations on food additives.

—to standardize the laws relating to flavorings so as to facilitate the free movement of food in the NAC nations while protecting health.

—to standardize laws relating to extraction solvents so as to facilitate the free movement of food in the NAC nations while protecting health.

—to include potassium acid sulphite (potassium bisulphite), which is used in wine production in the list of permitted preservatives. To fully authorize the use of thiabendazole.

—to extend the period of temporary authorization for certain emulsifiers, stabilizers, thickeners, and gelling agents.

—to standardize legislation on food starches in order to facilitate the free movement of foodstuffs within the NAC nations and to protect health.

—to supplement existing legislation on food packagings, wrappings, etc. by a regulation on contact materials.

—to implement legislation on plastic packing material to take account of technical progress in the field of migration tests.

—to standardize legislation on labelling of food to end national exemptions. This will improve the flow of information throughout the NAC nations, improve consumer awareness, and facilitate trade.

—to standardize food labelling requirements to include the percentage of alcohol in alcoholic drinks to ensure that consumers are adequately informed.

—to set out common rules for labelling alcoholic drinks. This will facilitate the free movement of these products within the NAC while ensuring that consumers receive adequate information about the origin, alcohol content, and certain other characteristics of products.

—to protect consumers against fraudulent labelling of food, and to allow exemption in order to meet specific nutritional objectives.

—to protect infant health by setting the compositional criteria for baby milks; by extending the rules relating to labelling, presentation, and advertising of foodstuffs for general consumption as necessary to cover these products.

—to provide for official inspections of food in order to protect the health and economic interests of consumers, while standardizing legislation which will facilitate the free movement of foodstuffs within the NAC nations.

—to allow the NAC authorized body to adopt methods for the sampling and analysis of food where necessary.

—to standardize NAC countries' laws on quick-frozen foods to facilitate their free movement within the NAC nations.

—to remove restrictions on the constituents of coffee and chicory products. This is to protect them from unfair competition from similar products manufactured outside the NAC nations.

—to standardize procedures on fruit juices in the light of technical developments in the production of some juices.

—to standardize procedures for fruit jams, jellies, and similar products in the light of technical developments in their production.

PHARMACEUTICALS

The NAC market for pharmaceuticals is unfortunately divided into distinct national markets. Although there are some loosely defined procedures impacting on the manufacture, testing, and marketing of pharmaceuticals and procedures for consultation among the national regulatory authorities, marketing authorizations remain national. National price control and social security refund systems also contribute to the partitioning of the markets.

There is a need for a unified market in pharmaceuticals, with NAC regulations on the marketing and development of medicines produced by bio-technology and the protection of highly innovative pharmaceutical products. Another critical area is that of pricing of pharmaceutical products and reimbursement by national social security schemes, along with communication on price controls. Also, regulations are needed to cover vaccines, products derived from human blood, radiopharmaceuticals used for diagnostic purposes, and generic medicines. Rules providing the guarantees of the quality of medicines and proper package information for patients are also desirable.

Regulations to eliminate obstacles to free circulation of pharmaceutical products within the NAC nations, the standardization of the conditions of distribution of pharmaceutical products to patients, and the provision of information to doctors and patients are sorely needed, along with rules for veterinary medicines to eliminate barriers to trade and improve the guarantees of safety for the animals treated and for consumers of foodstuffs of animal origin. Regulations needed in the pharmaceutical area are many but might include:

—to coordinate NAC nations procedures for authorizing high-technology medicines, especially those based on biotechnology. This will both protect public health and liberalize the NAC market in high-tech medical products.

—to adopt quicker procedures for making technical updates on the testing of pharmaceuticals.

—to adopt a quicker procedure for making technical updates of veterinary medicines and their testing.

—to adopt guidance measures for marketing of proprietary medicines to facilitate their movement within the NAC countries.

—to avoid repetitive testing on humans and animals by relaxing those requirements where similar products have already been authorized. Presently the inefficiency in this area is noted when seeking marketing authorization for new pharmaceutical producers who have to provide detailed results of tests performed, even though there may be many similar products already on the market.

—to ensure that products are available to all at reasonable prices and to control the cost of health services. This requires the standardization of such measures so that they do not constitute barriers to trade.

—to provide proper procedures for non-proprietary medicinal products. To improve the information available to consumers about medicinal products. To lay down certain provisions governing the export of medicinal products. To improve the guarantees of the quality of all medicinal products.

—to standardize proprietary medicinal products to include immunological medicinal products, allergen products, vaccines, toxins, and serums.

—to standardize proprietary medicinal products to include products derived from human blood.

—to standardize proprietary medicinal products to include radiopharmaceuticals.

CHEMICALS

Differing regulations for chemical products give rise to a multitude of problems. Divergent levels of health and safety protection are a clear obstacle to the creation of a NAC market. Free movement of chemical products throughout the NAC nations cannot be guaranteed if classification, packaging, and labelling requirements differ in the individual NAC countries.

In this area the emphasis is on protecting the health and safety of people and their environment and, at the same time, ensuring users that they are adequately provided with information about products placed on the market. In general, the NAC approach should be to adopt an umbrella regulation in a specific field, amending this from time to time to reflect technical progress. Regulations needed in the chemicals area are many but might include:

—to prohibit the marketing and use of PCBs and PCTs (polychlorinated biphenyls and polychlorinated terphenyls) except in special circumstances. Substitutes have been developed which are considered less dangerous to human beings and the environment.

—to prohibit the use of asbestos. This will ensure adequate public health protection throughout the NAC.

—to standardize national measures on classification, packaging, and labelling of dangerous preparations to facilitate the establishment of a common market and provide protection for public health.

—to set requirements on the minimum biodegradability level for certain detergents.

—to standardize the marketing of fertilizers, and to include liquid fertilizers.

—to standardize procedures on solid fertilizers to include their calcium, magnesium, sodium, and sulphur content.

CONSTRUCTION PRODUCTS

The construction sector raises problems of two kinds. Firstly, there is the problem of obstacles to the free movement between NAC nations of construction equipment. Secondly, there is the problem of differing standards for buildings, which can mean different levels of protection for occupants. The lack of common standards for construction equipment restricts manufacturers to national rather than NAC-wide markets. In order to promote their products throughout the NAC, costly modifications have to be made, frustrating the ideal of the internal market. As with motor vehicles and agricultural machinery, the lack of NAC type-approval procedures leads to repeated testing and certification of components. Costs mount and valuable resources are wasted.

Safety requirements are also essential not only for construction equipment but also for buildings. Safety in hotels is particularly important because of the number of persons at risk, particularly at night, and of the fact that many hotels are in older buildings. Regulations needed in the construction products area are many but might include:

—to standardize national legislation relating to tower cranes so as to remove differences that constitute trade barriers.

—to ensure that all hotels throughout the NAC countries are covered by minimum safety requirements.

PROTECTING THE CONSUMER

In many areas of the economy the lack of common standards and product regulations frustrates the creation of a unified market. Goods cannot move freely from one nation of the NAC to another, testing and certification procedures have to be repeated for each nation, and consumers are provided with varying levels of protection and information. Clearly the standardization of essential product regulations and procedures is necessary to create a truly common market, and to allow the NAC to become an effective force of competition in world markets. The emphasis must be on providing a high level of health and safety for all NAC citizens and to protect the environment.

Regulations are also needed:

—to ensure that the public get as much information as possible about the household products they are buying and aid the free movement of household appliances in the NAC.

—to standardize legislation relating to noise emissions from machinery so as to remove any barriers to trade that exist due to differences in national provisions.

—to ensure that laboratories in all nations of the NAC claiming to follow good laboratory practice are subject to regular controls by public authorities. This will allow for a mutual recognition of test results throughout the NAC, thus preventing the waste of valuable resources.

—to standardize all national legislation relating to the marketing of dangerous products resembling foodstuffs (e.g., toys looking like candy, toys looking like guns) which present a significant danger to children.

—to standardize the labelling of cosmetic products.

—to inform and protect consumers while liberalizing trade in food within the NAC nations by standardizing requirements for indicating unit prices on labels.

—to inform and protect consumers while liberalizing trade in non-food products within the NAC nations by standardizing the obligations to indicate reselling price and the unit price.

Progress in standardization will be of the utmost importance to the consumer, for it is in this area that protections are of paramount concern to them. Standardization in the NAC provides for upgrading in most areas affecting health, safety, confidence, trust, and psychological security.

17

A CHARTER OF SOCIAL RIGHTS

Full implementation of the Treaty within the New American Community must ultimately include a program for adjusting the social needs of workers to establish an equitable and consistent protection for all. Opposition to a system of equality throughout will come from many competing sources. Fears of jobs moving away from one nation to another will be a pressing issue. Likewise, poorer nations will resist economic and wage equity in that, they will argue, inequity would provide opportunities of fuller employment with hopes of raising living standards.

In spite of all the trials and tribulations that will inevitably be debated, legislation of basic social rights is required and would include the following rights.

FREEDOM OF MOVEMENT

A single labor market should encourage the mobility of labor such as the ability to take social security and state-private pension rights from one NAC nation to another. Let us remember that some nations at given periods of time have labor surpluses, others have labor shortages, and the two never match up because people don't move toward jobs. There is a permanent need to have a fluid exchange of skilled people moving about all over the NAC without any particularly significant net migratory movement.

Each worker of the NAC shall have the right to freedom of movement throughout the territory of the Community, subject to restrictions justified on grounds of public order, public safety, or public health. The right to freedom of movement shall enable any worker to engage in any occupation or profession in the NAC in accordance with the principles of equal treatment as regards access to employment, working conditions, and social protection in the host nation. The right of freedom of movement shall also imply: standardization of conditions of residence in all NAC nations, particularly those concerning family reunification; elimination of obstacles arising from the non-recognition of diplomas or equivalent occupational qualifications; and improvement of the living and working conditions of border workers.

EMPLOYMENT AND REMUNERATION

Every individual shall be free to choose and engage in an occupation according to the regulations governing each occupation. All employment shall be fairly remunerated. To this end, in accordance with arrangements applying in each country: workers shall be assured of an equitable wage, *i.e.*, a wage sufficient to enable them to have a decent standard of living; workers subject to terms of employment other than an open-ended, full-time contract shall benefit from an equitable reference wage; and wages may be withheld, seized, or transferred only in accordance with national law; such provisions should entail measures enabling the worker concerned to continue to enjoy the necessary means of subsistence for him or herself and his or her family. Every individual must be able to have access to public placement services free of charge.

LIVING AND WORKING CONDITIONS

The establishment of the NAC must lead to an improvement in the living and working conditions of people in the Community. This process must result from an approximation of these conditions while the improvement is being maintained, as regards in particular the duration and organization of working time and forms of employment other than open-ended contracts, such as fixed-term contracts, part-time working, temporary work, and seasonal work. The improvement must cover, where necessary, the development of certain aspects of employment regulations such as procedures for collective redundancies and those regarding bankruptcies.

Every worker of the NAC shall have a right to a weekly rest period and to an annual paid leave, the duration of which must be progressively standardized in accordance with national practices. The conditions of employment of every worker of the NAC shall be stipulated in laws, a collective agreement, or a contract of employment, according to arrangements applying in each nation.

SOCIAL PROTECTION

According to the arrangement applying in each nation every worker of the New American Community shall have a right to adequate social protection and shall, whatever his or her status and whatever the size of the undertaking in which he or she is employed, enjoy an adequate level of social security benefits. Persons who have been unable either to enter or re-enter the labor market and have no means of subsistence must be able to receive sufficient resources and social assistance in keeping with their particular situation.

FREEDOM OF ASSOCIATION AND COLLECTIVE BARGAINING

Employers and workers of the NAC shall have the right of association in order to constitute professional organizations or trade unions of their choice for the defense of their economic and social interests. Every employer and every worker shall have the freedom to join or not to join such organizations without any personal or occupational damage being thereby suffered by him or her.

Employers or employers' organizations, on the one hand, and workers' organizations, on the other, shall have the right to negotiate and conclude collective agreements under the conditions laid down by national legislation and practice. The dialogue between the two sides of industry must be developed and may, if the parties deem it desirable, result in contractual relations in particular at inter-occupational and sectoral level.

The right to resort to collective action in the event of a conflict of interest shall include the right to strike, subject to the obligations arising under national regulations and collective agreements. In order to facilitate the settlement of industrial disputes, the establishment and utilization at the appropriate levels of conciliation, mediation, and arbitration procedures should be encouraged in accordance with national practice. The internal legal order of member nations shall determine under which conditions and to what extent the rights apply to the armed forces, the police, and the civil service.

VOCATIONAL TRAINING

Every worker of the NAC must be able to have access to vocational training and to benefit therefrom throughout his or her working life. In the conditions governing access to such training there may be no discrimination on grounds of nationality. The competent public authorities, undertakings, or the two sides of industry, each within their own sphere of competence, should set up continuing and permanent training systems enabling every person to undergo retraining to improve his or her skills or to acquire new skills, particularly in the light of technical developments. Every worker of the NAC should have language training, as the biggest obstacle to moving or doing business across borders is language.

EQUAL TREATMENT FOR MEN AND WOMEN

Equal treatment for men and women must be assured. Equal opportunities for men and women must be developed. To this end, action should be intensified to ensure the implementation of the principle of equality between men and women as regards access to employment, remuneration, working conditions, social protection, education, vocational training, and career development. Measures should also be developed enabling men and women to reconcile their occupational and family obligations.

INFORMATION, CONSULTATION, AND PARTICIPATION FOR WORKERS

Information, consultation, and participation for workers must be developed along appropriate lines, taking account of the practices in force in the various member nations. This shall apply especially in companies or groups of firms having establishments or companies in two or more NAC member nations.

Such information, consultation, and participation must be implemented in due time, particularly in the following cases: when technological change which, from the point of view of working conditions and work organization, has major implications for the workforce, is introduced into undertakings; in connection with restructuring operations in undertakings or in cases of mergers having an impact on the employment of workers; in cases of collective redundancy procedures; when transborder workers in particular are affected by employment policies pursued by the undertaking where they are employed.

HEALTH PROTECTION AND SAFETY AT THE WORKPLACE

Every worker must enjoy satisfactory health and safety conditions in his or her working environment. Appropriate measures must be taken in order to achieve further standardization of conditions in this area while maintaining the improvements made. These measures shall take account, in particular, of the need for the training, information, consultation, and balanced participation of workers as regards the risks incurred and the steps taken to eliminate or reduce them.

PROTECTION OF CHILDREN AND ADOLESCENTS

Without prejudice to such rules as may be more favorable to young people, in particular those ensuring their preparation for work through vocational training, and subject to derogations limited to certain light work, the minimum employment age must not be lower than the minimum school-leaving age and, in any case, not lower than 15 years. Young people who are in gainful employment must receive equitable remuneration in accordance with national practice.

Appropriate measures must be taken to adjust labor regulations applicable to young workers so that their specific development and vocational training and access to employment needs are met. The duration of work must, in particular, be limited—without it being possible to circumvent this limitation through recourse to overtime—and night work prohibited in the case of workers under 18 years of age, save in the case of certain jobs laid down in national legislation or regulations. Following the end of compulsory education, young people must be entitled to receive initial vocational training of a sufficient duration to enable them to adapt to the requirements of their future working life; for young workers, such training should take place during working hours.

ELDERLY PERSONS

According to the arrangements applying in each country, every worker of the New American Community must, at the time of retirement, be able to enjoy resources affording him or her a decent standard of living. Any person who has reached retirement age but who is not entitled to a pension or who does not have other means of subsistence, must be entitled to sufficient resources and to medical and social assistance specifically suited to needs.

DISABLED PERSONS

All disabled persons, whatever the origin and nature of their disablement, must be entitled to additional concrete measures aimed at improving their social and professional integration. These measures must concern, in particular, according to the capacities of the beneficiaries, vocational training, ergonomics, accessibility, mobility, means of transport, and housing.

IMPLEMENTATION OF THE CHARTER

It is more particularly the responsibility of NAC nations, in accordance with national practices, notably through legislative measures or collective agreements, to guarantee the fundamental social rights in this Charter and to implement the social measures indispensable to a strategy of economic and social cohesion.

The truest and ultimate test of how effective the NAC will be rests with the successful implementation of a social rights program. Once accomplished (and there will be considerable pressure in all directions to both eliminate and/or water down these charter concepts), the score card for the NAC will indicate to the entire world that it has been responsive, responsible, and correct in having been formed. It shall be rewarded, in turn, by its happy, healthy, and proud citizenries.

18

THE VISION: "MADE IN THE NEW AMERICAN COMMUNITY"

"Made in the New American Community" is an idea whose time has arrived. It will come only after considerable argument, an abundance of heated debate, and then, some failures. The NAC will not evolve easily, as mistrusts and counter-accusations of imperialism, colonization, or loss of sovereignty will be heard time and again. The pull between protectionists and fair- free-traders will be severe. In the end, the fair- and free-traders will win out.

Institutional restructuring is difficult enough when it involves merging of organizations of differing products and values. No historic evidence, to date, has shown that it can more readily or more easily be done with independent nations, determined to hold on to their powers, governments, traditions, and cultural heritage. The battle over the formation of Europe in a post–1992 period provides adequate evidence of the discords that have and will continue to surface.

In spite of all this, the model of the NAC has its own advantages and, of course, a parallel set of disadvantages. The United States and Canada, though uneven in many ways, share a timely value system of open enterprise, cultural similarity, and traditional harmony. They in turn, combining with Mexico, create the first full stage of free-trade accords that will be the harbinger of the NAC. The NAC will initially involve only three nations, of which Mexico will represent the example of a lesser economy to start with, an explosive potential to follow. As this troika prospers and functions effectively, so will the remaining plan flower.

A successful launching of NAC will more than adequately communicate to the rest of the Americas that the idea for a common market can be realistic and productive. If Mexico illustrates to the other Latin American nations that she is able to benefit from the alliance with Canada and the United States without being swallowed or made to play a secondary role, then others will rush to participate.

LEARNING FROM HISTORY

Pitfalls will have to be avoided whenever possible. Lest we forget, prior to the European Community's proclaimed moment in history, January 1, 1993, the rhetoric in its closing months provided signs of a block to international trade rather than the flow of an international trade bloc. In the months before year's end 1990, E.C. actions were counter to the freer markets and deregulation goals at the nucleus of the 1992 project. As politicians were embellishing lofty visions, Europe had slipped backward into old habits of increasing state control of the economy, clubbish cronyism (wherein *what* you know continues to play second fiddle to *whom* you know), and egotistical self-obsession.

This trend was highlighted by the initial failure of the General Agreement on Tariffs and Trade in the closing month of 1990. The E.C. caused the breakdown by insisting on protecting its farmers and failing to grapple with its money-losing, and eventually unaffordable, state subsidies for agriculture. Many of Europe's and the world's savviest businesspeople realize that this protectionist bent, if continued, could easily boomerang and jeopardize Europe's unprecedented post-World War II economic prosperity as well.

The E.C.'s 12 member countries continue to act as separate nation-states, as distinct peoples, setting up alliances when possible, but concerned above all with their own national power and security. Centuries of European political philosophers have explored the organic relationship between a people and its government. If a government is not of a people, as well as for it, you have at best a useless bureaucracy, and at worst a dictatorship of a technocratic elite. Governments must move closer to the people, not further away from them.

Some of 1992's admirable goals were shoved aside. In place of the common market, there is an emphasis on political unification and the expansion of social regulations designed to protect the vested interests that 1992 was supposed to abolish. The original treaty of the E.C., its 1957 Treaty of Rome, relied on market forces to harmonize national economic differences. Unfortunately, this aim was being subverted by the old-line collectivists, who were exiled from the national politicals of their respective countries to join the bureaucracy of the E.C. seeking to expand its powers. The E.C.'s single market had become a pretext for political and social centralization. What must be discovered by the NAC leadership

that escaped those of the E.C. is how to evolve a supranational government. However attractive the ideal, multinational federations have proven
to be, in practice they exacerbated national resentments. The E.C. program of 1992 has had a history of being inherently divisive.

It is doubtful that the United States, as contrasted with Japan, will lose
very much from post–1992 in Europe. Protectionism, a continuing head-
ache for the Japanese and other Asian nations, should be of no particular
worry for us, because U.S. manufacturing affiliates and even wholesale
trade affiliates in the E.C. are largely independent of imports from the
U.S. For manufacturing affiliates, imports from the U.S. account for only
about 5 percent of sales in the European Community. Perhaps with time,
a structure of counterbalancing institutions will emerge to considerably
reduce the growing influence of nepotism and favoritism emerging within
the E.C.

POLITICAL UNION

The part of a future New American Community that most people may
find hardest to visualize is the idea of a NAC acting towards the outside
world with a united mind, a single will.

Though differing by degree throughout the hemisphere, New American
Community nations represent separate nationalisms. Although they have
diminished in strength, they have not disappeared, nor will they, nor
should they. People from differing countries display different feelings
toward their historic past, cultures, and fears of outside influence and
potential dominance.

The Gulf War in 1991 and the struggle in Yugoslavia have shown the
world, and more importantly, citizens of western Europe how frustrating
and difficult it is to cast an acceptable and unanimous foreign policy. The
December 1991 summit meeting in Maastricht, Holland evidenced the
tensions and complexities of forging a political union, strengthened by a
common, united federal bond. In the end political unification may not
only become the stumbling block to a truly functioning New American
Community, but it may embarrass all involved nations into realizing that
any capacity to speak and act as one is still almost entirely theoretical.

A WORD OF CAUTION

Organizationally, the NAC will require a home base, established phys-
ically in one country (rotation on a pre-set basis is impractical and inefficient). The dedication of the employed bureaucrats must be centered on
their loyalties to the NAC and not to their individual nation. Every effort
should be made to minimize the tempting growth of employees who will

be needed to run the NAC. Obviously, many people will be required to translate the weighty documents that will evolve. Unlike the nine languages of E.C. activities, the NAC will commence with only three (English, Spanish, and French) and, when fully extended, have a fourth (Portuguese). Inevitably, the NAC, with the passage of time, will create and disseminate its own lexicon, but this should be kept to a minimum.

The ever-presence of greed will tempt the weak. The center of the NAC and its decision-makers will welcome visitors with all types of agendas, hidden and revealed. Plenipotentiaries will visit, along with solicitors and attorneys who will come to plead, to set their own careers on a stronger path and legitimacy. The nucleus of the NAC will sort itself out as a babble of languages, replete with headphoned translators, an intrusion of governmental representatives, the shuttle of ministers and diplomats, well-paid lawyers, an aviary of pressure groups and advisors, all pushing ideas forward in praise of progress.

If the European Community's preparation for 1992 is a predictor of the NAC evolution then lobbying will become one of the NAC's major by-products. We must avoid the thousands of lobbyists surrounding headquarters representing thousands of firms and trade associations all busily seeking access to thousands of bureaucrats, parliamentarians, and commissioners. The petitioners have a tremendous motive to bend the deliberations toward their views, or to the views of their sponsors, with much to gain or lose, depending on how a single market develops.

Within the evolution of the NAC there also will be a fight of multinational firms on all fronts. Individually they will tug each other for an upper hand politically and an increased market share. Jointly, they will coalesce to battle the government and public-interest groups over what they consider to be too stringent standards, rules, and restrictions.

In addition, politicians often vote not by conscience, but instead are swayed by their ability to influence, thus they are by nature influenced by others. In the evolution of the NAC, leaders (since they will be selected by the people they are properly, though perhaps regrettably, also politicians) must be accountable each step of the way, and instead of pretending to know what they are doing, be reminded of their obligation that they indeed do know what they are doing, and what the implications of their actions can be. The collective leadership should be wary of agreeing to things they don't fully understand, or of taking actions the long-term consequences of which they cannot foresee.

The cost of failure to implement multinational free-trade accords with a Latin American common market would be high. For the first time in decades, these regions are democratic and committed to sensible economic reform. Failure to initiate these efforts might topple friendly leaders, undermine new democracies, and weaken cooperation. It could also jeopardize efforts to restructure Latin American economies along free-market, export-oriented lines. A commitment and a love affair with our own hemisphere countries should be as profound as those we have provided with other global nations.

As free-trade zone accords are negotiated among the NAC nations, government and corporate officials must resist the temptation to bash Japan, or any other country that attempts to fairly manipulate their own free-trade interests. Cracking down on exports from competing non-NAC companies with harassment or other non-productive strategies will not necessarily benefit consumers on either side of the conflict.

Although Japan's trade surplus with the U.S. was \$42 billion in 1991, up 10 percent from 1990's \$38 billion her export-import balance with the U.S. has actually changed little. Americans did purchase more Japanese products during the year, but many of them were being made in plants within U.S. boundaries.

It is vital that we realize and accept that Japan, in part, works in a different system, with a host of different premises. Other ways of manipulating an economy, derived from cultural differences, will certainly yield economic inconsistencies.

The United States and Japan do not share all the same systems and values. All parties must accept such variances which inevitably lead to conflict. Image makers must stop attempting to mold Japan into a U.S. model; we would not tolerate such manipulation. Political and company handlers of any nation do however have the right (and responsibility) to protect the economic interests of their country. At the same time, a sound argument can be made for allowing certain industries to decline and ultimately collapse, as world-wide competition forces us out of the marketplace. Establishing or maintaining tariff barriers will not solve the hysteria of any nation.

Our value system has evolved from a western concern for the natural rights of man. Indeed, historically the U.S. ethic has produced numerous arguments for tariff-free borders. Seventeenth century English philosopher John Locke's *Second Treatise on Government* elaborated on individuals' natural rights where " . . . every man has a property in his own person. This nobody has any right to but himself. The labour of his body and the work of his hands, we may say, are properly his." Locke's emphasis on the individual as the unit of action, as the entity who thinks, feels, chooses, and acts followed from his perception of natural law thus forming the natural rights of people. He offered one of the best moral lessons for free trade.

The prose of America's abolitionist William Lloyd Garrison, found in his *Declaration of Sentiments* of the American Anti-Slavery Convention in December 1833 flamed: "The right to enjoy liberty is inalienable. . . . Every man has a right to his own body—to the products of his own labor— to the protection of law. . . . That all these laws which are now in force, admitting the right of slavery, are, therefore, before God, utterly null and void . . . and therefore they ought instantly to be abrogated.'' This bold phrase reinforces the principle of a free movement for both goods and people.

Increased prosperity traditionally parallels the lowering of tariffs. U.S. tariffs have been declining since 1890 when the average tariff rate was 48.4 percent. By 1950 it had dropped to 12.0 percent, 1960 to 11.8 percent, 1970 to 7.4 percent, 1980 to 5.5 percent, and 1989 to 5 percent.

Those who argue against free trade would be wise to reflect on the statement of Henry George, famous for his single tax, who more than 100 years ago penned:

Free trade consists simply in letting people buy and sell as they want to buy and sell. It is protection that requires force, for it consists in preventing people from doing what they want to do. Protective tariffs are as much applications of force as are blockading squadrons, and their objective is the same—to prevent trade. The difference between the two is that blockading squadrons are a means whereby nations seek to prevent their enemies from trading; protective tariffs are a means whereby nations attempt to prevent their own people from trading. What protection teaches us is to do to ourselves in time of peace what enemies seek to do to us in time of war.

First must come the series of free-trade accords. This step is the harbinger to the common market. Along the way, fiscal and trade barriers will fall, common standards will be set, educational priorities and avenues will be encouraged, merger and industrial cooperation will settle in, services of all types will be made available with equality as the golden rule, health to individuals and to the environment shall surface as the singular priority, social rights for all will be the banner command, and political unity will enshrine itself as the collective force and presence before the world-at-large. The effort will be rewarded, the hemispheres will combine as a force to be taken seriously, as a dynamic example of what can be created. Disunity will submit to an order of a heightened living standard. The quest for improving tomorrow over yesterday will arrive.

Ever expanding, other countries throughout Central and South America, and the nation islands will clamor to enter the common market of the NAC. The evidence of benefit will outweigh all the questioning and criticism. In a short time, Alaska to Chile will be entwined into a colossus of supreme management and harmony, paving the way in the new millennium to a centrifugal force of unparalleled envy and advance.

For the New American Community to have a chance of success involves a significant degree of mutual trust and influence between NAC nations. Once set in place, the New American Community will slowly surface and move out away from its secure buildings to test itself in the open field. At that time the great experiment will gather speed.

REFERENCES

Introduction

Nasar, Sylvia. "Boom in Manufactured Exports Provides Hope for U.S. Economy." *The New York Times*, 21 April 1991.

Chapter 1

Baldwin, Richard. "The Growth Effects of 1992." *Economic Policy*, October 1989.

Baldwin, Robert E., Carl B. Hamilton, and Andre Sapir. *Issues in U.S.-E.C. Trade Relations*. National Bureau of Economic Research Conference Report. Chicago: University of Chicago Press, 1988.

Barber, Lionel. "A Future Scenario?" *Europe*, July/August 1990.

Bayne, Nicholas. "Making Sense of Western Economic Policies: The Role of the OECD." *The World Today* 43, February 1987.

Brown, Donna. "Game-Winning Strategies for Europe's New Market." *Management Review*, May 1990.

Cecchini, Paolo. *The European Challenge–1992: The Benefits of a Single Market*. Commission of the European Communities. Newcastle-upon-Tyne: Wildwood House, Ltd., 1988.

Ernst & Whinney. "Europe 1992: The Single Market." 1988.

Hoffman, Stanley. "The European Community and 1992." *Foreign Affairs*, Fall 1989.

Krause, Axel. "1992's Impact on American Business Accelerates." *Europe*, June 1989.

"Lest a Fortress Arise." *The Economist*, 26 October 1991.

"Pact Expands Europe's Common Market." *The Wall Street Journal*. 23 October 1991.

Revsin, Phillip. "Brussels Babel." *The Wall Street Journal*, 17 May 1989.

Rosenberg, Jerry M. "Europe 1992 and Technological R & D." *SuperConnections* 3, no. 2, Summer 1990.

————. *The New Europe: An A to Z Compendium on the European Community*. Washington, D.C.: Bureau of National Affairs, 1991.

————. "The Fall of U.S. and the Rise of E.C. Research and Development." In *The Challenge of a New European Architecture: Implications for the European Community's Internal and External Agendas*. Center for European Community Studies, Arlington, VA: George Mason University, 1991.

Chapter 2

Bradsher, Keith. "Chip Pact Set by U.S. and Japan." *The New York Times*, 4 June 1991.

"Business Week." *The Economist*, 13 April 1991.

Dore, Ronald. *Taking Japan Seriously*. London: The Athlone Press, 1987.

Frankel, Jeffrey. "Is a Yen Bloc Forming in Pacific Asia?" *Amex Bank Review*, November 1991.

Fromm, Joseph. "Pacific Rim: America's New Frontier." *U.S. News and World Report*, August 1984.

Greenhouse, Steven. "Europeans United to Compete with Japan and U.S." *The New York Times*, 21 August 1989.

Higashi, C., and G. Peter Lauter. *The Internationalization of the Japanese Economy*. Boston: Kluwer Academic Publishers, 1990.

Ishihara, S. *The Japan That Can Say No*. New York: Simon & Schuster, 1991.

"Japan's Economic Power Surges in the Region." *The Wall Street Journal*, 26 March 1991.

Lincoln, Edward J. *Japan: Facing Economic Maturity*. Washington, D.C.: The Brookings Institution, 1988.

Metraux, Daniel. *The Japanese Economy and the American Businessman*. Lewiston, NY: Edwin Mellen Press, 1989.

Ohmae, Kenichi. "Japan's Rice-Paddy: Protectionism Begins on the Farm, and the Farmers Have the Votes." *Washington Post*, 3 May 1987.

Russell, George. "Trade Face-Off: A Dangerous U.S.-Japan Confrontation." *Time*, 12 April 1987.

Sanger, David E. "Japan to Allow Foreigners' Bids." *The New York Times*, 2 June 1991.

Ueda, Hideaki. "Look at the Trade Deficit with Japan—It's Melting." *Business Week*, 25 March 1991.

United States, International Trade Commission. "The Effects of Greater Economic Integration within the European Community on the United States." Publication 2318. Washington: GPO, 1990.

Van Agt, A. "How Japan is Changing." *Europe*, May 1990.

Weiss, Julian. "Asia Prepares for 1992." *Europe*, October 1989.

Chapter 3

Bethell, Leslie. *The Independence of Latin America*. New York: Cambridge University Press, 1987.

The European Community and Central America. Brussels: Europe Information-External Relations, 1981.

The European Community and Latin America. Brussels: Europe Information-External Relations, 1985.

The European Community's Relations with Latin America. External Relations, Commission of the European Communities, December 1989.

Fajnzylber, Fernando. *Industrialization in Latin America: From the Black Box to the Empty Box*. New York: United Nations, no. 60, 1990.

Friedman, George, and Meredith Lebard. *The Coming War with Japan*. New York: St. Martin's Press, 1991.

New Trade and Economic Relations between Brazil and the European Community. Brussels: Europe Information-External Relations, 1982.

Rashish, Peter S. "Stepping Up E.C. Assistance Programs." *Europe*, November 1991.

Thirteen Years of Development Cooperation with the Developing Countries of Latin America and Asia. Brussels: Commission of the European Communities, 10 May 1989.

"World Investment Report 1991: the Triad in Foreign Direct Investment." UNCTC, United Nations, 1991.

Chapter 4

The Economic Evolution of Japan and Its Impact on Latin America. Economic Commission for Latin America and the Caribbean. Santiago, Chile: United Nations, 1990.

Foreign Direct Investment in Latin America: Recent Trends, Prospects and Policy Issues. New York: United Nations, Series A, no. 3, UNCTC, August 1986.

Ministry of International Trade and Industry. "Japan's Direct Overseas Investment in FY 1986." *News from MITI*, June 1987.

Sterngold, James. "Japan Retreating on Promised Loans." *The New York Times*, 14 April 1991.

"Why Japan Inc. Is Steering Clear of Mexico." *Business Week*, 2 December 1991.

Chapter 5

Barcelo, John J., III. "Subsidies and Countervailing Duties—Analysis and a Proposal." *Law and Policy in International Business* 9, 1977.

Bereuter, Doug. "Farm Trade: A U.S. Viewpoint." *Europe*, April 1986.

Bhagwati, Jagdish. *The World Trading System at Risk*. Princeton: Princeton University Press, 1991.

Bonker, Don. *America's Trade Crisis: The Making of the U.S. Trade Deficit*. Boston: Houghton Mifflin Co., 1988.

Curtis, Kenneth, and John Carroll. *Canadian-American Relations: The Promise and the Challenge*. Lexington, MA: Lexington Books, 1983.

Davey, Keith. *Canada Not For Sale: The Case against Free Trade*. Toronto: General Paperbacks, 1987.

Farnsworth, Clyde H. "U.S. Cautions Europe on Protectionism." *The New York Times*, 6 October 1989.

Kellner, Irwin L. "Why Our Trade Gap Persists." *Manufacturers Hanover Economic Report*, September 1986.

Kuttner, Robert. *The End of Laissez-Faire: National Purpose and the Global Economy after the Cold War*. New York: Knopf, 1991.

Lee, Susan. "Are We Building New Berlin Walls?" *Forbes*, 7 January 1991.

McCracken, Paul. "Toward World Economic Disintegration." *The Wall Street Journal*, 9 February 1987.

Office of the U.S. Trade Representative. " 'Super 301' Trade Liberalization." Washington, D.C., 25 May 1989.

Roberts, Steven V. "Congress Chiefs Warn of Action to Curb Trade." *The New York Times*, 5 September 1985.

Samuels, Franks E., Jr. "Ease Up on Export Controls." *Washington Post*, 17 November 1986.

Sinclair, Ward. "The World Doesn't Need Our Farmers." *Washington Post*, 29 December 1985.

Chapter 6

Asman, David. "The Salinas Reforms Take Root." *The Wall Street Journal*, 2 December 1991.

Auerbach, Stuart. "Business Won't Fight Trade Bill." *Washington Post*, 12 June 1986.

Becker, Gary S. "As Nations Splinter, Global Markets Are Merging." *Business Week*, 22 April 1991.

"Bolivia: On The Forefront of Reform." *The New York Times*, 6 May 1991.

Brooke, James. "Latin Armies Are Looking for Work." *The New York Times*, 24 March 1991.

———. "Feeding on 19th Century Conditions, Cholera Spreads in Latin America." *The New York Times*, 21 April 1991.

———. "Peru Struggles to Digest Free-Market Reforms." *The New York Times*, 30 April 1991.

———. "In Brazil, Pessimism Starts to Keep Pace with Inflation Rate." *The New York Times*, 1 December 1991.

Burns, E. Bradford. *Latin America: A Concise Interpretive History*. New Jersey: Prentice Hall, Inc., 1990.

Burns, John F. "Trade Pact Foes Rally in Canada." *The New York Times*, 6 April 1987.

"The Business of the American Hemisphere." *The Economist*, 24 August 1991.

Daremblum, Jaime. "Mexico Becoming a Window of Opportunity for Central America." *The Wall Street Journal*, 15 March 1991.

Dornbusch, Rudiger. "Dornbusch on Trade." *The Economist*, 4 May 1991.

Farnsworth, Clyde H. "Concerns Raised on Mexican Trade." *The New York Times*, 20 February 1991.

———. "Bush Trade Concessions Pick Up Some Support." *The New York Times*, 2 May 1991.

Golden, Tim. "Mexican Trade Pact Advances." *The New York Times*, 28 October 1991.

———. "Mexican President Outlines Program for Changes." *The New York Times*, 2 November 1991.

Junco, Alejandro. "The Case for an Internal Mexican Free-Trade Agreement."
    The New York Times, 22 March 1991.

Kirland, Lane. "The Free-Trade Myth Is Ruining Us." *The New York Times*, 26
    September 1986.

"Latin-American Debt: Catching Up." *The Economist*, 13 April 1991.

"Latin American Integration—Getting Together." *The Economist*, 31 March
    1991.

"Latin America's Economic Reforms." *The Economist*, 19 October 1991.

Main, Jeremy. "How Latin America Is Opening Up." *Fortune*, 8 April 1991.

"Mexico Beckons, Protectionists Quaver." *The Economist*, 20 April 1991.

Moffett, Matt. "For Mexico, Prospects Are Appealing." *The Wall Street Journal*,
    22 April 1991.

———. "U.S., Mexico, Canada Seek to Revive Trade Talks." *The Wall Street
    Journal*, 24 October 1991.

Munck, Ronaldo. *Latin America: The Transition to Democracy*. New Jersey: Zed
    Books, Ltd, 1989.

Nash, Nathaniel C. "Terrorism Jolts a Prospering Chile." *The New York Times*,
    9 April 1991.

———. "A New Discipline in Economics Brings Change to Latin America." *The
    New York Times*, 13 November 1991.

Ortiz de Zevallos, Felipe. "New Peruvian Finance Minister Preaches Free-Market
    Gospel." *The Wall Street Journal*, 29 March 1991.

Palmer, Jay. "The Debt-Bomb Threat." *Time*, 10 January 1983.

Pressman, Steven. "Trade Relief Program Target of Revival Effort." *Congres-
    sional Quarterly*, 18 January 1986.

"Privatisation in Latin America." *The Economist*, 23 March 1991.

Reilly, William K. "Mexico's Environment Will Improve With Free Trade." *The
    Wall Street Journal*, 19 April 1991.

Rosenbaum, David E. "Trade Issues Enter Crucial Political Phase." *The New
    York Times*, 9 April 1991.

Suro, Roberto. "Border Boom's Dirty Residue Imperils U.S.-Mexico Trade."
    The New York Times, 31 March 1991.

Taylor, George Holding. "Chile Can Win on Fast Track." *The Wall Street Journal*,
    1 November 1991.

"Trade-block Folly."*The Economist*, 20 April 1991.

Wertman, Patricia, and William Cooper. "The Latin American Debt Crisis and
    U.S. Trade." *Congressional Research Service Report for Congress*, No.
    87–19E, 14 January 1987.

Wessel, David. "A High-Stakes Battle for an Integrated Market." *The Wall Street
    Journal*, 22 April 1991.

Wonnacott, Paul. "The United States and Canada: The Quest for Free Trade:
    An Examination of Selected Issues." *Policy Analysis in International Eco-
    nomics*, 16. Washington, D.C.: Institute for International Economics,
    March 1987.

Chapter 7

Colchester, N., and D. Buchan. *Europower: The Essential Guide to Europe's
    Economic Transformation in 1992*. New York: Random House, 1990.

Europe: Magazine of the European Community (various issues). Washington, D.C.: Delegation of the Commission of the European Communities.

Silva, M., and B. Sjogren. *Europe 1992 and the New World Power Game*. New York: J. Wiley, 1990.

Truitt, Nancy S. "Latin Bishops Look for Liberation in a Market Economy." *The Wall Street Journal*, 10 May 1991.

Chapter 8

Bulletin of the European Communities, Supplements. Belgium: Commission of the European Communities.

The Court of Justice of the European Community. Luxembourg: European Documentation, Periodical 5, 1986.

European Unification: The Origins and Growth of the European Community. Luxembourg: European Documentation, Periodical 1, January 1990.

A Journey Through the E.C. Brussels-Luxembourg: Commission of the European Communities, 1986.

Noel, Emile. *Working Together: The Institutions of the European Community*. Luxembourg, 1988.

Wallace, Cly. *Corporate Handbook to the European Community*. New York: United States Council for International Business, May 1990.

Chapter 9

The ABC of Community Law. Luxembourg: European Documentation, Periodical 2, 1986.

European Community News. New York: E.C. Office of Press & Public Affairs.

European Information-External Relations. Brussels: Commission of the European Communities.

Winter, Audrey. *Europe without Frontiers: A Lawyer's Guide*. Washington, D.C.: Bureau of National Affairs, 1989.

Chapter 10

Antel, Vivienne M. "Achieving Success in the Global Arena." *Europe*, November 1989.

The Elimination of Frontier Barriers and Fiscal Controls. Commission of the European Communities, Ernst & Whinney, March 1988.

The Removal of Technical Barriers to Trade. Luxembourg: European File, Commission of the European Communities, November 1988.

Chapter 11

Education and Training in the Approach to 1992. Luxembourg: European File, Commission of the European Communities, April 1990.

Education Training Youth. Brussels: Commission of the European Communities, 1989.

European Documentation. Federal Republic of Germany: Commission of the European Communities, Periodicals.

European File. Brussels: Commission of the European Communities.

Social Europe: The Labor Market for Information Technology Professionals in

Europe. Luxembourg: Commission of the European Communities, January 1990.

Chapter 12

Behr, Peter. "Coalition Growing to Boost Level of U.S. Competitiveness." *Washington Post*, 5 October 1986.
Conditions for Industrial Cooperation. Brussels: Commission of the European Communities, Ernst & Whinney, March 1988.

Chapter 13

Dodge, Elaine, and Christy Law. "Poisoned Meat from Canada." *The New York Times*, 31 May 1991.
Plant & Animal Health Controls. Brussels: Commission of the European Communities, Ernst & Whinney, March 1988.
Simons, Marlise. "The Message to Europe: Don't Mess with Cheese." *The New York Times*, 29 November 1991.

Chapter 14

Banco Central do Brasil. *Boletim Mensual* 22, no. 8, August 1986.
A Common Market for Services. Brussels: Commission of the European Communities, Ernst & Whinney, March 1988.
Europe 1992 and the Insurance Industry. The Netherlands: KPMG, 1989.
A European Financial Area: The Liberalization of Capital Movements. Luxembourg: European File, Commission of the European Communities, June/July 1988.
Kapstein, Jonathan, and Patrick Oster. "Why Europe Is in Dollar Shock." *Business Week*, 4 March 1991.
"Telecommunications: The New Highways for the Single European Market." Luxembourg: Commission of the European Communities, October 1988.

Chapter 15

Bylinsky, Gene. "The Higher Tech Race: Who's Ahead." *Fortune*, 13 October 1986.
Europe 1992 and the High Technology Industry. UK: KPMG, 1989.
The European Community of Research and Technology. Luxembourg: Commission of the European Communities, 1987.
The European Community's Research Policy. Luxembourg: European Documentation, Periodical 2, 1985.
Krickau-Richter, Lieselotte, and Otto von Schwerin. *E.C. Research Funding*. Germany: Commission of the European Communities, January 1990.
Peterson, Thane. "Can Europe Catch Up in the High-Tech Race?" *Business Week*, 23 October 1989.
Research and Technological Development for Europe. Brussels: European File, Commission of the European Communities, December 1987.
Research and Technological Development Policy, Luxembourg: European Documentation, Periodical 2, 1988.

Chapter 16

Finan, William F., Perry D. Quick, and Karen M. Sandberg. *The U.S. Trade Position in High Technology: 1980–1986*. Washington, D.C.: Quick, Finan and Associates, October 1986.

Jones, Norman. "A Strategy for Revitalizing Industry." *Business Week*, 3 March 1986.

A New Community Standards Policy. Brussels: Commission of the European Communities, Ernst & Whinney, March 1988.

"Standardization in Information Technology and Telecommunications." Brussels: Commission of the European Communities, October 1987.

Chapter 17

Basic Community Social Rights. Brussels: European Communities, Economic and Social Committee, February 1989.

The Community Charter of Fundamental Social Rights for Workers. Luxembourg: Commission of the European Communities, May 1990.

Health and Safety at Work in the European Community. Luxembourg: European File, Commission of the European Communities, March 1990.

A Human Face for Europe. Luxembourg: European Documentation, Office for Official Publications of the European Communities, 1990.

The Social Policy of the European Community: Looking Ahead to 1992. Luxembourg: European File, Commission of the European Communities, August/September 1988.

Venturini, P. *1992: The European Social Dimension*. Brussels: Commission of the European Communities, 1990.

Chapter 18

"Annual Report of the President of the United States on the Trade Agreements Program." Washington, D.C.: Government Printing Office, 1990.

Bernstein, Aaron. "Warning: The Standard of Living Is Slipping." *Business Week*, 20 April 1987.

Fliess, Barbara. "Working Toward Closer Ties." *Europe*, September 1989.

"Forget Pearl Harbour." *The Economist*, 30 November 1991.

George, Henry. *Protection or Free Trade*, 1886. Reprint Edition, New York: Robert Schalkenbach Foundation, 1980.

Kiplinger, A.H., and Kiplinger, K.A. *America in the Global '90s*. Washington, D.C.: Kiplinger Books, 1989.

Mallabre, Alfred L., Jr. "U.S. Economy Grows Ever More Vulnerable to Foreign Influences." *The Wall Street Journal*, 27 October 1986.

Thurow, Lester C. "A World-Class Economy: Getting Back into the Ring." *Technology Review 88*, August/September 1985.

INDEX

ABOUT THE AUTHOR

JERRY M. ROSENBERG is Professor of Management at the Graduate School of Management at Rutgers University in New Jersey. He has authored 14 books and dictionaries, including *Inside the Wall Street Journal* (1982), *The Investor's Dictionary* (1986), *Dictionary of Information Technology and Computer Acronyms, Initials, and Abbreviations* (1991), and *The New Europe* (1991).